COPYRIGHT NOTICE

Printed in the United States of America

CARPE VINUM

Wine, wine, wine
A fine and rare invention!
To satisfy my passion
Let us drink its juice divine.
Shame to him who will not sip
Nor press the nectar to his lip.

from *Canadians of Old*
by Philippe Aubert de Gaspé

Contents

About the Authors

Erin and Courtney Henderson are The Wine Sisters — sister sommeliers and co-directors of a Toronto-based wine events and touring company. Realizing the want and need for customized, private wine tours and professional yet fun wine tasting experiences, Erin and Courtney joined forces and responded to the demand.

Prior to creating "The Wine Sisters," Erin and Courtney served at some of Toronto's leading venues. Well-informed and patriotically-enthusiastic about the region, Courtney developed and maintained an Ontario-only wine list during her tenure at the Art Gallery of Ontario, and led the "Great Canadian VQA (Vintners Quality Alliance) Search" while at the Fairmont Royal York Hotel, a judging for the best local wines to make up her wine list. (VQA is Ontario's regulatory and appellation system which guarantees wine quality and authenticity, similar France's AOC system).

Erin curated Ontario-focused wine lists as a sommelier at a private Toronto club, introducing members to the exceptional quality of regional bottles by leading tasting events and inviting local winemakers to take part in 100-kilometer dinners.

The sisters now happily continue to advocate Ontario wines in their tastings and tours, though luckily, their clients don't really need much convincing and often request experiences based on local wines.

In addition to hosting wine tastings, hospitality training, party planning, and leading private tours through wine country, The Wine Sisters have a strong presence in the media. Along with writing wine reviews for Canada's national wine magazine, *Vines*, their wine writing has been featured in theloop.ca, Huffington Post, and *Wine in Canada*, a special Maclean's publication focusing on the Canadian wine industry. In 2015, The Wine Sisters hosted WineTalk Radio, a weekly call-in radio show on NewsTalk 1010 in Toronto, increasing attention for local wines among both the wine trade and consumers.

Erin and Courtney are wine and spirit instructors at Toronto's George Brown College in Toronto and wine judges for Intervin (an international competition of wine available to the Canadian market). They have also led tutored wine tastings at the Gourmet Food and Wine Show in Toronto as well as Savour Stratford.

To visit their popular blog or for more information, visit www.thewinesisters.com or follow them on Twitter @TheWineSisters.

Introduction

"Adventure is just bad planning."
— Roald Amundsen, Polar Explorer

They say good things come to those who wait, but that's never been our experience. There is no better time than the present to discover the acres of vineyards, winemaking traditions, culinary treats, and more in Lake Ontario wine country.

Whether visitor or native, we're going to assume that your time is valuable, so in this practical, user-friendly format we've decided to show you how to make the most of a day trip or long weekend with the kind of fresh and knowing information that could only come from the familiarity of two sisters who eat, sip, and breath this place. We'll see to it that your pilgrimage to wine country is less a freelance "adventure" and more an efficient, rewarding experience — both in efficiencies of travel and getting to the good stuff without wasting time on the unnecessary.

It appears we're not the only impatient wine travelers; late last year Greater Toronto Airways (www.flygta.com) began flying twice daily from downtown Toronto's Billy Bishop Airport to Niagara-on-the-Lake, cutting a two-hour drive to a very civilized 12-minute flight. Affordable, seamless and certainly luxurious, seats on the small charters sell fast, so if time is of the essence, book well in advance.

Niagara has almost 100 wineries between the Escarpment and Niagara-on-the-Lake, and Prince Edward County more than 35. That's a lot of ground to cover, so it's always helpful if you have a guide — virtual or otherwise — to help you focus.

Ontario is a cool climate region, similar to Burgundy, New York or Germany (though technically we're on the same latitude as Mendocino County in California and Chianti Classico in Italy). That means we typically produce focused, fresh, balanced wines with higher acidity and lower alcohol, making them food friendly, interesting and complex.

While Ontario is probably best known for Icewine (see page 8), the world is also coming to know and love our elegant and focused Chardonnay, Pinot Noir, Riesling, and Cabernet Franc (and we, personally, we would like to add Gamay to that list). However, Ontario actually produces nearly 50 quality varietal wines, including spicy Syrah and mineral-driven Pinot Gris plus the styles of Icewine (yes, one word and capitalized — we've trademarked it!), and traditional method sparkling wine.

Icewine may have put Ontario on the world stage, but the aforementioned wines are what have helped keep us there. And winemakers — both new and veteran — continue to push boundaries, experimenting (usually successfully) with new styles like the currently en vogue orange wine, robust appassimento or wild ferments.

As you sip your way around Lake Ontario, you may notice VQA (Vintner's Quality Alliance) on bottle labels. VQA is our local governing wine body, and amongst other things, ensures that the grapes inside are all at least from Ontario — and in cases where you see a sub-appellation designation, from that specific area.

Our favourite time to visit wine country is the Fall, when the leaves are changing, the harvest is in full swing, and the multitudes of peak-season tourists have thinned out. The winter is also beautiful, a white wonderland where wineries celebrate the season by hosting outdoor marshmallow roasts, opening a community skating rink, or even the occasional horse-drawn sleigh ride offering. If you are visiting in the off-season, however, make sure to call in advance as many wineries reduce their hours, or even shut down altogether.

Of course, the high season in summer offers terrific energy, as city dwellers escape to the romantic, vineyard-laced country sides of Niagara and Prince Edward County. Almost all wineries are family- and dog-friendly (just double check before visiting), and many feature outdoor eating areas, patios and restaurants, so it's fun to relax with a glass of something cool and crisp with a plate of a local cheese while people-watching. A word of warning: weekends in the summer can get very, very busy, so while hospitality is always warm and genuine, bustling workers may not have a lot of time to chat. If you're looking for some special attention, plan your visit during the week.

Rest assured, no matter the season, there is always something going on to make your road trip an enlightened experience. Visitors will find wine region attractions like fine restaurants, country inns, villages, hiking trails and cultural events (see Calendar of Events on page 171).

Carole King crooned that life is a tapestry, and that's certainly true for Canada's Lake Ontario wine country. Consider the book you hold in your hands as our personal invitation to the amazing tapestry of the region. Read on, wine traveler, as you begin your journey to this slice of viticultural heaven.

Erin and Courtney Henderson
www.thewinesisters.com

Overview

Lake Ontario was formed about 12,000 years ago when the ice sheet covering much of North America receded and meltwater filled the basins gouged out by glaciers. Among indigenous tribes of the region, it was the Wayandots who called the lake "Onitariio," their word for "lake of shining waters."

Canada's winemaking history dates back to Johann Schiller, a German who served with the 29th infantry regiment of the British Army in repulsing the American Revolutionary attempts to capture Quebec. When his regiment returned to England, Schiller petitioned for bounty land and was granted a 400-acre parcel in Toronto Township. With techniques learned in his native Rhine valley, he began growing grapes, making wines, and sharing bottles with his neighbours.

In the early 1860s, Schiller's sons sold the property to an aristocratic Frenchman, Count Justin de Courtenay, who established Chateau Clair, the first commercial vineyard and winery in Canada. His prize-winning wines at the 1867 Paris Exposition inspired others to follow, and by 1890 there were 41 commercial wineries in Canada, 35 of them in Ontario.

Like the United States, Canada endured a "dry period" in the consumption of alcohol, and although Ontario-made wines remained legal during that period, quality was ignored in favor of quantity, as the number of wineries in the region more than doubled, from twenty to fifty-one. Then, with the formation of the Ontario Wine Standards Committee and a preoccupation with improving quality, it would be several decades before a new winery was licensed in Ontario. Things began to normalize in 1979 when Inniskillin was granted the first commercial winery license in nearly 50 years..

Today, Ontario has three major wine regions: Prince Edward County, above and across Lake Ontario from Rochester, New York; Niagara, just west of Buffalo, New York; and Lake Erie North Shore, on the other side of Lake Erie from Cleveland, Ohio.

In this guide, we focus on two of the three: Niagara, Ontario's largest and most popular wine region, and Prince Edward County (PEC), the province's newest official region.

PEC (or The County as it is locally known) started to attract winemakers and investors in 2000, and steadily grew until earning official appellations status from VQA (Vintner's Quality Alliance, Ontario's governing wine body). It now has more than 35 wineries, and the people keep coming.

Surrounded by the Bay of Quinte and Lake Ontario, The County is almost an island, known for serious limestone soils (a là Burgundy), that's filled with fossilized shellfish from millennia ago when the whole area was covered in water. This prized soil is what gives County wines an unmistakable minerality. Of course there's also the weather. PEC has a climate so cool vines need to be buried in the fall to avoid damage from the harsh winter. It's a painstaking process, but a worthwhile one as grapes like Chardonnay and Pinot Noir are flourishing.

Travel west for about 5 hours and you'll arrive at the Niagara Peninsula which is further broken up further into two main regions: Niagara-on-the-Lake and the Niagara Escarpment, the latter being what locals refer to as "The Bench."

Within those two appellations, there are about 10 sub-appellations, which have been defined by the VQA as areas with unique geographical characteristics and therefore warrant the special demarcation, areas that typify grape character and the distinctive imprint of origin.

Lake Ontario wine country — throughout the Bench and NOTL — is very easy to navigate. Signage is excellent, and even if you do lose your way, you can hardly swing a dead grape vine without hitting a cluster of wineries ready and waiting to greet you with warmth and hospitality.

For many years it was believed that vitis vinifera grapes could not survive the rigors of Canadian winters and the freeze-thaw-freeze cycle of early spring. As a result, the majority of plantings in Ontario were the winter-hardy North American labrusca varieties (such as Concord and Niagara, and early-ripening, winter-resistant hybrids, such as Vidal, Seyval Blanc, Baco Noir and Marechal Foch.

However, Lake Ontario, with an average depth of 86 metres, is slow to cool down and heat up, keeping the region milder in winter and cooler in the summer heat. The surface area and depth give the lake a large heat storage capacity that responds slowly to winter air temperatures, and from early April to the end of September, the surface temperature of the lake is cooler than the surrounding land temperature. Breezes circulating between the lake and the Escarpment enhance this moderating effect. With Lake Ontario to one side, and the protected slopes to the other, Niagara's winemakers have ultimately proved the region uniquely situated for the production of world-class wines.

In recent years the region has attracted international media who've been impressed with our little slice of the wine world, and gone home to report about its magic. *The Boston Globe, The New York Times, Wine Spectator* and *Decanter* are just a few who have run features on why our wines, restaurants and scenery are worth a visit.

Visitors will sometimes call the whole area "Niagara Falls" and while it's a direct neighbour, and a famous one at that, Niagara Falls is not wine country. Still, we would be remiss not to include a visit this natural wonder. It's a tourist mecca for a reason, and worth a brief stop to take a picture and buy the t-shirt.

·

The Icewine Story

In the late 1940s, the Vidal Blanc grape was brought to Canada by Adhemar de Chaunac, a French-born Canadian enologist working for the Ontario wine producer T.G. Bright & Company. De Chaunac was responsible for bringing many hybrid varieties to Canada to determine which grapes could grow well in the Canadian climate. He was the first to experiment with the German Eiswein method, leaving the grapes to freeze on the vines well into winter. Vidal is now the most common Icewine grape in Ontario, producing wines which routinely win international competitions.

The first commercial Canadian Icewine was made in 1978 by Hainle Vineyards in British Columbia. Ontario followed in 1984, when Karl Kaiser of Inniskillin produced his first batch, using nets to protect the sweet grapes from hungry foraging critters.

Between the end of the growing season and harvest, the grapes dehydrate, concentrating their juices. While still frozen, harvested grapes are pressed, leaving most of the water behind as ice. Only a small amount of concentrated juice is extracted. Juice yields for Icewine grapes are much lower than for table wines — only 15% of the expected yield for traditional table wines.

Besides Vidal, Icewines in Ontario are now made from other thick-skinned white grape varieties such as Riesling and Gewurztraminer, although red varieties such as Cabernet Franc have been turned into Icewine. These wines are luscious and intensely-flavoured, boasting rich aromas and flavours of ripe tropical fruits (such as lychee, papaya and pineapple). All varietals are sweet, but with a firm backbone of acidity, making them perfectly balanced.

Serve Icewine on its own after a meal as a digestive. The rule is to pair this rich, sweet wine with a dessert that is a bit lighter and less sweet, or with something savoury and full-flavoured for balance. Try it with a simple dessert of fresh fruit with cheese.

Although traditionally served in smaller glasses, Icewines benefit from a regular white wine glass, which showcases all of its wonderful aromas. Because the sugar content is high, Icewines will retain their vigor for three to five days after opening if stored in the refrigerator.

Cold winter and warm summer seasons make Ontario the only production region to yield Icewine every year across the world.

Niagara Peninsula

The two major appellations making up the Niagara Peninsula are Niagara Escarpment and Niagara-on-the-Lake (NOTL). Within those major appellations are 10 smaller, sub-appellations, demarcated for their unique microclimates, soils and topography.

The Niagara Escarpment, or what locals call "The Bench," runs from west of St. Catharines to Grimsby and produces fresh, mineral-driven wines thanks in part to the escarpment's frost protection and air circulation. Deep soils and sloping vineyards provide not only steady moisture to vines but also good drainage.

Niagara-on-the-Lake provides a mix of soils, elevation and microclimates (it's not uncommon to have several degrees difference in temperature in vineyards that are only a few kilometres apart), though all sub-appellations enjoy the moderating effects of the deep waters of Lake Ontario and the fast flowing Niagara River.

Prince Edward County

With a growing season a month or two shorter than Niagara's, early-ripening varieties — particularly Chardonnay and Pinot Noir — predominate in Prince Edward County. The foundation of this appellation is what geologists call the "Trenton Limestone Plateau," remnants of an ancient seabed formed by billions of fossilized shelled creatures that give wines an unmistakable minerality. Stony soils allow for excellent drainage in the spring and acts like a wet sponge throughout the growing season, forcing vines to grow deeper during the hot summer months and produce small yields with concentrated flavours.

Growers face a big challenge every winter when temperatures can dip below -24C, the point at which buds on the vines will die. To protect them, workers "hill up" the vines after harvesting the grapes in the fall and bury them under the soil, which provides enough insulation to keep them alive over the winter. In the spring, they undertake the mammoth task of de-hilling the vines, removing the soil and uncovering the vines. It's a delicate task that must be done by hand to prevent damage.

Tasting Etiquette

There are not a lot of rules for enjoying a great glass of wine, but there are some ways you can make your winery visits more enjoyable for both you and other visitors. Follow these tips to maximize your experience.

Tasting rooms provide sample tastings, poured by trained staffs whose primary concern is your education and enjoyment of their products. At a few stops you will meet some of our most important winemakers.

Many tasting rooms are open year-round, typically seven days a week. Peak tourist season begins in June and runs through October, and in the off-season, expect shorter hours, mainly on weekends, or by appointment only. Wine tastings are usually not available on holidays such as Canada Day, Labour Day, Thanksgiving, Christmas and Boxing Day. The more popular wineries can be crowded, especially during the tourist season, which means less individual attention. You might consider a weekday visit if it fits your schedule. Crowds diminish substantially and pourers have more time to talk shop.

Call in advance if your group will be larger than five. Some of the smaller wineries don't have space for buses or limousines. Others like to know in advance if large groups will be arriving so they can provide enough staff. Always make an appointment where indicated — if the winery sign reads "By Appointment Only," don't pop in unannounced. Most of the time all it takes is a quick phone call to arrange a visit. Be prepared to show a valid form of I.D.

A successful tasting room experience begins with preparation. Start the day with a good breakfast and continue to snack throughout the day. Make sure you're hydrated before leaving home. Drinking water between each tasting will have little benefit if you're starting out with an empty (water) tank. Pack plenty of bottled water for your trip and drink often. Take along a large cooler. If you buy wines on your trip, you'll need a place to store them during the day. Tossing them in a hot trunk may "cook" them before you get them home.

Proper tasting requires the ability to experience the aroma or bouquet of the wines. Wearing perfume, cologne, after-shave, sun tan lotion, or even chapstick or lipstick can interfere with your full appreciation of the aromatics, and with that of other visitors in the tasting room. Minimize the use of anything that might have a distracting scent. No chewing gum or smoking. And skip the coffee. One cup will kill your palate for a good half hour.

There is no cost for admission to tasting rooms, although most wineries require a fee to taste the offerings. When a fee is charged, it's okay for two people to share the same glass and pay only one tasting fee. Tasting fees will sometimes be deducted from the price of the wine, and a few wineries will include a souvenir glass with the fee.

Don't crowd the tasting counter. If you arrive at a busy tasting bar, await your turn, then back away from the bar after receiving your next tasting to give others a chance to progress in their tasting order. Keep your cell phone on vibrate. Step outside if it is necessary to use your phone so as not to disturb others.

Most wineries will have a detailed list of wines they'd like you to try. But keep in mind, you do not have to taste every wine on the list, in fact, it often makes more sense to ignore a winery's full offering, focus on a particular varietal, or cherry-pick as few as one or two wines per stop. You may, for instance, decide to taste only Riesling and Icewine, sampling just those at each winery. This technique can help you learn how different vineyards, different vintages, and different winemakers affect the finished wine.

Recommendations throughout this book will help to identify specific proficiencies and best bottles without being overwhelmed. Visiting a winery knowing exactly what you want to taste identifies you as a more confident and better educated consumer. You will likely receive special attention and have the standard tasting fee waived.

Keep in mind that you are in a tasting room, not a bar. Only a small amount of wine — usually an ounce — will be poured into your glass. Correct wine etiquette does not dictate that you must finish every tasting portion. Taste buds wear out easily.

The most basic rule is to drink white wine before red, and always dry before sweet. Always save late harvest and Icewines for last. Wine sampling is about finding the flavors that you enjoy the most, and you are never wrong when it comes to choosing wines that you enjoy. Taste each wine carefully and savor each sip.

If a winery provides tasting notes, read as you taste and see if you recognize any of the aromas or flavors listed in the notes. (Descriptors at the back of this book will help you put words to the aromas and flavors you're tasting). Bring your own notebook and keep track of what you like about each wine. Taking notes not only helps you to remember what you tasted, but it's a signal to attentive pourers that you are serious about the tasting exercise. This will often get you a bit more personalized treatment.

Rinsing your glass is a good idea when the tasting moves from whites to reds or to dessert wines. Some wineries discourage rinsing with water as it can affect the next wine and they'll insist on rinsing it for you with little wine.

The sense of smell is one of the most sophisticated of all the senses. In order to get the true bouquet of a wine, begin by swirling. To properly swirl, place the glass flat on the table, hold it by the stem, and rotate it in a circle to aerate the wine. Then stick your nose right in there — it's been suggested that a sense of smell may be more than ten thousand times more sensitive than that of taste. To skip the aroma or bouquet of a wine is to deprive yourself of an important part of the pleasure. (Don't swirl sparkling wines; bubbles already provide proper aeration).

Once in your mouth, roll the wine around so that it coats the front, back, and side of your tongue. This is when professional tasters refer to the wine on their palate. Slowly savoring a small amount of each wine you sample not only helps maintain sobriety, it also helps you fully appreciate each wine. Drinking water between sips helps in this regard. Use the spit bucket. That's what it's there for. Use it even if you have a designated driver. Don't be afraid to dump the wine once you've tasted it, your pourer will not be offended and will recognize your empty glass as a signal to pour the next taste. In crowded tasting rooms, or where buckets are too full for comfort, request a paper or plastic cup for more discreet spitting.

Under ordinary circumstances, asking for a second taste of one particular wine is inappropriate. However, if you're sincerely interested in buying the wine, let the pourer know your intentions.

You are under no obligation to buy wine at the tasting room. However, if you fall in love with a wine, by all means buy it at the winery. Many winery tasting rooms are pouring wines not available elsewhere. Smaller production wineries have limited distribution, and their wines can be difficult (or impossible) to find in a wine shop or liquor store. You can typically buy by the bottle or by the case (12 bottles). Wineries will often apply a case discount (and sometimes a half-case discount), mixed or matched.

The time spent in a tasting room or winery is a time for discovery and learning. Ask questions. Most tasting room personnel are very knowledgeable about the wine, winery and vineyards. Their explanations, descriptions, and stories can add to your appreciation of their wines. The key to learning about wine is tasting, so try out new wines you haven't had before and keep educating your palette until you learn what you like.

No one under the age of 19 may sample wine. Since they won't be allowed to taste wines, young children may find the tasting-room experience tedious. For this reason, some wineries discourage (but usually don't prohibit) kids. If you plan to bring your kids along on a trip to wine country, have planned activities for them while you are tasting. They can become easily bored. Keep them away from breakable objects in the tasting room.

You are allowed to bring Canadian wines across the border into the U.S., but it's best to check at the border crossing for the latest rules and regulations. There is no limit on the number of bottles purchased for personal use, however, they may be subject to nominal fees for duty and taxes. Keep receipts for all your purchases, and tell the inspector exactly how many bottles you have in the car.

.

How to Use This Book

Finding, trying and retaining information about new wines can be overwhelming for even the most ardent traveler, let alone planning for meals along the way and comforting accommodations at the end of the day.

In this guide you will find our personal recommendations for places to visit, sleep, eat and sip. If we were in your car with you, these are the exact places we would go, and the exact things we would do. We've listed two separate itineraries for both one day and weekend wine tasting trips (and a separate guide to scenic and historic sites) for visitors who begin travel from either Toronto or crossing from the US into Canada through Buffalo.

Within the limitations of either day trip or a weekend tour, we've carefully plotted driving directions, selecting high points from a well-informed insider's view and making it possible to get from one place to the next in a reasonably allotted time. Travelers who have more days to spend may want to supplement this guide with more comprehensive information available from winery Internet sites.

To begin, choose the section based on your starting point, then select the length of your visit. Your schedule should not be set in stone. The best experiences include "must-visits" mixed in with some flexibility, and some will prefer to travel at their own pace and take their own detours. Permission granted.

This book is intended to be user-friendly. Mark it up, underline, and make notes along the way. Extra space has been allowed at the end of each section for that purpose.

Please Note: From early spring through late fall, most wineries will be open to the public throughout the day (usually from 10 AM to 5 PM). During the off-season, days and hours of operation vary greatly from winery to winery, so phone ahead to inquire about tasting opportunities. Of course, always call ahead for dinner reservations and plan in advance for overnight accommodations .

Section 1: Niagara Wine Trails/Wineries

Section 2: Niagara Wine Trails/Wineries (Alternate)

Section 3: Prince Edward County Wine Trails/Wineries

Section 4: Scenic and Historic Points of Interest

Notes

Entry Point:

TORONTO

WINE TRAILS

DAY TRIP

>*From downtown Toronto the drive will take about 90 minutes to 2 hours without traffic. Take the Gardiner Expressway west for about 5 kilometres (3 miles), continuing as it turns into the QEW west. After about 50 km (31 miles), keep left at the fork to stay on the QEW towards Niagara. Continue another 40 km (25 miles) taking exit 57 toward Victoria Ave. Turn right onto Marina Blvd., turn right onto Victoria Avenue, left on to Vadere Avenue, left onto Vanguard Road, continuing onto Valentine, continuing onto Vista Avenue. Foreign Affair is on your right.*

THE FOREIGN AFFAIR WINERY

4890 Victoria Avenue North, Lincoln
Phone: 905-562-9898
Online: www.foreignatfairwinery.com

This winery can be a bit tough to find tucked in behind the Vineland research centre, but it's worth seeking out. The large moose statue should help guide you. Homey and welcoming, this boutique winery was founded by Len and Marissa Crispino (who sold it last year to Corby, the Canadian subsidiary of Pernod Ricard). It was inspired by their love of Italy, and more specifically the appassimento wine making style of Amarone. They were among the first in the area to start working with the unique wine making technique, and for their efforts won an award for innovation from the province.

Insider's Tip: The family's love of both Italy and Canada are captured on the wine labels. All show an Italian countryside, but each wine has a different iconic Canadian animal roaming the Italian backdrop.

>*Take Victoria Avenue South; turn right onto King Street. Kacaba is about 600 meters ahead on the left.*

KACABA

3550 King Street, Lincoln
Phone: 866-522-2228
Online: www.kacaba.com

Kacaba offers oodles of charm and serious wine country hospitality. To keep your visit personal and personable, tours around the tiny winery are for you or your group only. Nothing is off limits, and visitors experience a working winery, especially exciting during fall harvest when things are really bustling. Specializing in big, full-bodied reds, the Syrahs and Cab Francs are not to be missed.

Insider's Tip: Visitors can try tank samples with discounted "futures" pricing available. When ready, bottles are shipped where applicable, or held indefinitely at the winery for pick-up

>Turn left onto King Street, follow the road for 1 km, taking a left onto Cherry Avenue. Tawse is 1km further on the left.

TAWSE WINERY

3955 Cherry Avenue, Vineland
Phone: 905-562-9500
Online: www.tawsewinery.ca

Tawse (pronounced like "paws" but with a "T") only opened to the public in 2005, but quickly shot to fame as one of Ontario's top wineries. Owner Moray Tawse, who also has holdings in Argentina and France, was intent on sparing no expense to create premium, age-worthy wines that could hold their own against any in the world. In fact, Moray has hosted cellar dinners, pitting his Pinots against famed Burgundies in blind tastings. Committed to organic and biodynamic, winemaker Paul Pender focuses on the land, dividing vineyards in blocks to get a true sense of the terroir. There are 65 labels in total, but top wines include Riesling, Cabernet Franc, Pinot Noir and Chardonnay.

Insider's Tip: If those wine-filled cellar dinners sound like fun, get on the mailing list, they're usually only advertised that way and often sell out in minutes.

> Turn left on Cherry Ave., turn left onto Moyer Road. Vineland is about 700 meters on the right.

VINELAND ESTATES WINERY

3620 Moyer Road, Vineland
Phone: 888-846-3526
Online: www.vineland.com

Stop at Vineland Estates for lunch. The winery restaurant was one of the first in Niagara and has been voted among the Top 100 restaurants in Canada. The property dates back to the 1800s when it was a Mennonite farm, and the original structures are still standing. The dining room is located in the farmhouse and the stunning boutique and tasting room are housed in a barn with massive wood beams, fully restored in 1999. Known for producing zesty, vibrant Rieslings, enjoy a glass with the cuisine of Chef Justin Downes.

Insider's Tip: The winery is said to be haunted with the spirit of the farming family's Grandma. We've taken tours there where guests have had odd things happen; ask about these strange occurrences when you visit.

> Turn right on Moyer Road., turn right onto Victoria Avenue, turn left onto Sixth Avenue and follow for about 1.4km.

BALL'S FALLS

3292 Sixth Avenue, Lincoln
Phone: 905-562-5235
Online: www.npca.ca

A perfect spot to stretch your legs and enjoy a dose of spectacular scenery, Ball's Falls is named after the Ball family, United Empire Loyalists who moved to the area in the early 19th century. Part of the land they purchased had two waterfalls — the upper falls and the lower falls – both of which can be viewed from above or below. Nature lovers will also enjoy bird-watching and hiking through the protected area, now in the care of Niagara Peninsula Conservation Authority.

> Take the QEW to Niagara, exit Regional Road 48/Niagara Street, keeping right at the fork. Turn left onto Niagara St., right onto Lakeshore Road, right onto Irvine Road.

SMALL TALK VINEYARDS

1242 Irvine Road, Niagara-on-the-Lake
Phone: 905-935-3535
Online: www.smalltalkvineyards.com

Whimsical and laid-back, Small Talk may be "boutique," but the winery makes a big splash with a brightly-coloured entrance and energetic hospitality. On land that's been farmed since the 1950s, visitors can get an inside look by jumping on a wagon for a guided tour of the grounds. Small Talk makes white, red and Icewine, but has recently started producing Shiny Apple Cider, crafted from estate-grown fruit.

Insider's Tip: Visitors love Small Talk's range of Icewines – Vidal, Riesling, and Cabernet Sauvignon.

> Head north on Irvine Road toward Lakeshore Road. Turn right and follow for about 4km. Konzelmann will be on your left.

KONZELMANN ESTATE WINERY

1096 Lakeshore Road, Niagara-on-the-Lake
Phone: 905-935-2866
Online: www.konzelmann.ca

With a long and storied history, Konzelmann has winemaking roots in Germany, dating back several generations. In 1984, the family set up shop in Niagara-on-the-Lake, becoming only the seventh winery to hang out a shingle. And it's quite the shingle — winery looks like the country stead of German aristocrats.

Insider's Tip: If you're a fan of fruit wines, Konzelmann makes a peach wine that is very popular with visitors.

> Go left on Lakeshore Road for 1.5 km, turn right onto Four Mile Creek, Turn left onto Hunter Road. Big Head Winery is on your left.

BIG HEAD

304 Hunter Road, Niagara-on-the-Lake
Phone: 905-359-3239
Online: www.bigheadwines.ca

You can't get much more up-close and personal to a working winery than Big Head. Visitors make their way through the machinery and equipment of a winery's usually-off limits areas to get to the bright red door of the tasting room. Inside, the immaculate, bright, white room — which doubles as the barrel cellar — is set up with a tasting bar for quick sampling and high-top tables for a more intimate one-on-one sommelier-led experience. Big Head is owned and operated by famed Niagara winemaker Andre Lipinski (who has worked and consulted at easily half a dozen wineries across the region) and his family. Son Jakub is head of operations and daughter Kaja manages events and hospitality. A fan of the concentrated appassimento style of wine making, Lipinski's reds and whites are simultaneously concentrated and generous but also focused and elegant.

Insider's Tip: The sommelier-led tastings are blind in an effort to give visitors an unbiased and open minded approach to the wines. It's worth the experience, but in high season it's best to book a week in advance, off season at least a day.

> *Turn left on Hunter Road. Turn left onto Niagara Stone Road. Turn right onto Mary Street. (Backhouse is in the plaza at the corner of Niagara Stone Road and Mary Street).*

BACKHOUSE

242 Mary Street, Niagara-on-the-Lake
Phone: 289-272-1242
Online: www.backhouse.xyz

Set in the unlikely location of a strip mall is where you'll find Niagara's newest, coolest restaurant. With the look of a modern Scandinavian farmhouse, replete with fur throws, wood piles and animal bone centre pieces, Backhouse is at once sleek and comfy, homey yet industrial. Created by husband-and-wife team Bev Hotchkiss and chef Ryan Crawford, the inventive menu focuses on "cool climate cuisine," with most components sourced locally and many from the on-staff farmer. Items are so fresh that offerings change daily depending on what's available and in season at the farm.

Insider's Tip: In true Canadiana fashion, guests are served a complimentary roasted marshmallow at the end of the meal, but if you are part of the last seating, guests are invited to the open kitchen to roast their own.

> *Turn right on Mary Street., turn left onto King Street., turn right onto Ricardo Street, then left onto Melville Street.*

PILLAR AND POST INN 🛏

48 John Street W., Niagara-on-the-Lake

Phone: 905-468-2123
Online: www.vintage-hotels.com

Tuck in here for the night. Only 800 metres from Backhouse, you can get in a short walk after a hearty dinner. The Pillar and Post Inn is so charming, some locals suggest a few guests have never left (as noted in the book, *Ghosts of Niagara-on-the-Lake*). Originally a cannery built in the 1800s, the stately hotel houses 122 rooms decorated in modern country chic, complete with exposed beams and brick.

Insider's Tip: Play a game of stare-eyes with the portrait of Lt. Col. John Butler hanging in the lounge.

Notes

Entry Point:

TORONTO

WINE TRAILS

WEEKEND TOUR

Friday

> *From downtown Toronto the drive will take about 90 minutes to 2 hours without traffic. Take the Gardiner Expressway west for about 5 kilometres (3 miles), continuing as it turns into the QEW west. After about 50 km (31 miles), keep left at the fork to stay on the QEW towards Niagara. Continue another 40 km (25 miles) taking exit 57 toward Victoria Avenue Turn right onto Marina Blvd., continuing onto Twenty-First Street, turn right onto Main Street. Inn on the Twenty is on your left.*

CAVE SPRING & ON THE TWENTY RESTAURANT

3836 Main Street, Jordan
Phone: 905-562-3581
Online: www.cavespring.ca

Drive into pretty Jordan Village for your first night. Check into The Inn on the Twenty, then walk across the street to visit Cave Spring, arguably the most famous producer of Riesling in Niagara, with a portfolio ranging from dry to sweet Late Harvest and Icewine. The 30-year-old winery also makes very good, well-priced reds and other white varietals. After the tasting, make your way next door to the exceptional On the Twenty Restaurant, where Chef Jason Williams keeps his focus on local cuisine.

Insider's Tip: Don't miss the "CSV" Riesling, a terroir-driven wine, hand-crafted from Cave Spring's oldest vines.

INN ON THE TWENTY

3845 Main Street, Jordan
Phone: 800-228-2801
Online: www.innonthetwenty.com

Inn on the Twenty is a charming, 24-suite boutique hotel in the heart of Jordan Village. A tasteful mix of antique and contemporary decor fill the serene, well-serviced Inn. An adjoining spa makes this an ideal destination for romantic getaways. Free wi-fi, parking, and dog friendly suites are available.

Insider's Tip: Traveling with a larger group? Check out the Wine Maker's Cottage or Vintage House.

Saturday

INN ON THE TWENTY

3845 Main Street, Jordan
Phone: 800-701-8074
Online: www.innonthetwenty.com

Enjoy a tasty breakfast overlooking wooded Twenty Valley before heading out for the day.

> *Head left on Main Street; turn left onto King Street/Regional Road 81; turn right onto Nineteenth Street, then left onto Seventh Avenue. Flat Rock is 2km further on your left.*

FLAT ROCK CELLARS

2727 Seventh Avenue, Jordan
Phone: 855-994-8994
Online: www.flatrockcellars.com

Flat Rock only does a handful of wines — Riesling, Pinot Noir, Chardonnay and Pinot-based Rosé — but that concentration on a small portfolio allows them to do those wines really well. Welcoming and hospitable, the hexagon-shaped, environmentally-sustainable building has floor-to-ceiling glass windows in its boutique, allowing visitors a view of the surrounding vineyards, and, on a clear day, the Toronto skyline from across Lake Ontario.

Insider's Tip: If you call in advance, owner Ed Madronich will personally guide your tour.

> *Take a left on Seventh Avenue, turn right onto Seventeenth Street, then left onto Staff Avenue.*

SUE-ANN STAFF ESTATE WINERY

3210 Staff Avenue, Lincoln
Phone: 905-562-1719
Online: www.sue-annstaff.com

The Staff family acquired this property 200 years ago, and has been growing grapes on the land for past century, but it wasn't until 2009 that Sue-Ann (of the fifth generation) began producing her own wines. With a small, tightly knit portfolio, the big news over the last few years has been the launch of the "Fancy Farm Girl" series which features both a red and white blend, rosé and traditional method bubbly.

Insider's Tip: Sue-Ann Staff was named "Winemaker of the Year" in 2002 by the Ontario Wine Society and is a recipient of the International Wine and Spirits Award in London, England as one of the top four "Women in Wine" in the world.

> **Turn left on Staff Avenue, then left onto Seventeenth Street.**

WESTCOTT VINEYARDS

3180 Seventeenth Street, Jordan Station
Phone: 905-562-7517
Online: www.westcottvineyards.com

Grant and Carolyn Westcott opened their namesake winery in 2014 after retiring from corporate life. Daughter Victoria runs the retail side and son Garrett assists in the vineyard. Specializing in Chardonnay and Pinot Noir, visitors to this elegantly rustic winery can order a flight (or just a glass) and chill out on the back deck while overlooking the vineyards. On site caterers Zooma provide an ample supply of indulgent treats like lobster grilled cheese or duck confit poutine from an ever-changing menu.

Insider's Tip: Food is provided by Bolete, the St Catharines-based restaurant which has taken Niagara region by storm with its local, well crafted menu.

> **Turn left on Seventeenth Street, then left onto Eighth Avenue. Eighth turns into Pelham Road. Continue about 5km to the winery.**

HENRY OF PELHAM FAMILY ESTATE WINERY

1469 Pelham Road, St. Catharines
Phone: 905-684-8423
Online: www.henryofpelham.com

Henry of Pelham has one of the most engaging stories of tragedy and triumph in Niagara. It was started in the 1980s by Paul Speck Sr. who recruited his three teenaged sons to work weekends, doing everything from planting vines to mopping floors. As the business began to take off, Paul Sr. passed away, leaving the fledgling winery to the boys, then in their early twenties and teen years. Fast forward 30 years and Henry of Pelham is still family owned and operated by Paul Jr., Matthew and Daniel Speck, who have grown it into a large boutique winery, making somewhere in the ballpark of 100,000 cases a year of premium VQA wines, exported around the world. Despite the success, the winery hasn't lost its welcoming, homey feel; three charmingly rustic buildings sit on the property, the tasting room and boutique, a seasonal restaurant, and a magnificent underground barrel cellar, which runs a story deep and is carved out of the exposed limestone and lined with towering rows of hundreds of barrels.

Insider's Tip: Henry of Pelham has the best Baco Noir in the province (reminiscent of a wine from the northern Rhone); and don't miss the traditional method sparkling, Cuvée Catharine Brut Rosé.

> *Turn left on Pelham Road, staying to the right to say on Pelham Road. Turn right on Glendale Avenue, turn left on Glenridge Avenue, turn left on Westchester Avenue, and continue onto Ontario Street. Turn right onto Church Street and left onto Wellington Street. Wellington Court is a Victorian House on the left.*

WELLINGTON COURT 🍴

11 Wellington Street, St. Catherines
Phone: 905-682-5518
Online: www.wellington-court.com

If you happen to be visiting wine country during the weekend when HOP's restaurant is closed, then head to the source! Wellington Court has been a staple of wine country casual-fine dining for more than 20 years. Located in downtown St Catharines just minutes from the vineyards of wine country, the restaurant started as a café in the 80s by Chef Erik Peacock's mother, and he took over the kitchen in the early 90s, growing Wellington Court into the popular restaurant it is now.

Insider's Tip: A delicious and indulgent snack menu is available from between lunch and dinner.

> *Turn right on Wellington Street, right onto Church Street, and left onto Ontario Street, continuing onto Westchester Avenue. Turn right onto Queenston Street, and left onto Niagara Stone Road. Southbrook is about 3.5km on the right side.*

SOUTHBROOK VINEYARDS

581 Niagara Stone Road, Niagara-on-the-Lake
Phone: 888-581-1581
Online: www.southbrook.com

With its iconic, long blue wall jutting from the winery, Southbrook is a beacon on Niagara Stone Road. It was Niagara's first Demeter-certified, biodynamic winery. It's also organic, and wines are vegetarian and vegan -friendly. Evidence of the terroir-focused attention is everywhere at this progressive enterprise. Sheep help maintain the grassy headlands and fertilize the ground; pigs are raised in a large, enclosed area that straddles farmland and forest, allowing them to roam far and wide and feast on acorns. This year, horse and wagon rides are offered to guests during the warm months for an insider's view of a working winery-farm. With advanced booking, visitors can take part in the "Earthly Infused Tasting" pairing four of Southbrook's wines to four (local and organic) small dishes. If you show up without a reservation, you can sample local cheeses at the tasting bar for only a few dollars or grab a bite on the patio.

Insider's Tip: Don't leave without trying Southbrook's Madeira-inspired fortified wine, "The Anniversary," or the natural Orange Wine, fast becoming the wine world's latest craze.

> *Take a right on Niagara Stone Road. Wayne Gretzky's is on your right.*

WAYNE GRETZKY ESTATES WINERY & DISTILLERY

1219 Niagara Stone Road, Niagara-on-the-Lake
Phone: 844-643-7799
Online: www.gretzkyestateswines.com

Wine and hockey lovers in the know, know that The Great One has had his own wine label for years, though fans have never had a dedicated winery to sample and sip 99's products. That all changes this year with the spring opening of Wayne Gretzky's Winery and Distillery - which adds to the wine portfolio premium Canadian ryes and other spirits. The venue will also host Niagara's first cocktail bar and a spectacular water feature — that, of course, changes to an ice rink in winter.

Insider's Tip: While skating around the rink, keep an eye out for the Loonie Gretzky buried at centre ice.

> *Take a right on Niagara Stone Rd. Silversmith is on your right.*

SILVERSMITH BREWING COMPANY

1523 Niagara Stone Road, Niagara-on-the-Lake
Phone: 905-468-8447
Online: www.silversmithbrewing.com

Stop for a pint at Silversmith. Housed in an old, vine-covered church that sits between a strip mall and a car dealership, the signage is small, though if you're visiting in summer you may see the umbrellas open on patio. The slightly incognito location hasn't hurt the craft brewery as it seems to be pretty full most days, and while we've never visited on a weekend, we're told seats are at a premium by noon. The kitchen is open daily for lunch and dinner, catered by MASON. The menu features global dishes created with "thoughtfully sourced" ingredients.

Insider's Tip: They run tours and tastings on the weekend, but like their seats, the tours are also in high demand so booking ahead is a good idea.

> *Turn right on Niagara Stone Rd. follow it to the end. Turn right on Queen St and drive for about 1km. Turn left on Victoria St. Pieza' is on the right.*

PIEZA' PIZZERIA

188 Victoria Street, Niagara-on-the-Lake
Phone: 289-868-9191
Online: www.piezapizzeria.com

The newest restaurant to hand out its shingle in the Historic Old Town of NOTL is a welcome edition indeed, featuring Napoli-styled pizzas home-made and wood fired in a gigantic oven imported from Europe. Bright and laid back, this welcoming pizza place is hopping most days.

Insider's Tip: The house-marinated vegetables, featured on the antipasto plate are a must-try.

> Head southeast on Queen St (toward the clock tower), turn left on King Street. Turn right on Ricardo Street, then left on Melville Street. Harbour House is on the corner.

HARBOUR HOUSE HOTEL 🛏️

85 Melville Street, Niagara-on-the-Lake
Phone: 866-277-6677
Online: www.niagarasfinest.com

This 4-Diamond Hotel, located across from the marina, artfully blends luxury with small town charm. From the chocolates and personalized stationary in your room, to the rubber ducky on the side of the Jacuzzi tub and complimentary afternoon wine and cheese pairings, Harbour House is at once comfy and elegant.

Insider's Tip: While there's no gym onsite, guests have access to the facilities at sister hotel Shaw Club, just up the street.

Sunday

STAGECOACH RESTAURANT 🍴

45 Queen Street, Niagara-on-the-Lake
Phone: 905-468-3133
Online: www.facebook.com/stagecoach-restaurant

A true old-fashioned diner, there are long queues for a decent breakfast at this classic greasy spoon. Fast, friendly service dishes up eggs, bacon and sausages, pancakes and potatoes. It may not be fancy, but it's solid diner grub that gets you in and out quickly.

Insider's Tip: We're not kidding about the lines – they stretch on to the sidewalk on weekend mornings, so get there early to beat the rush.

> Take a left onto Ricardo Street. Ricardo bends to the right and turns into John Street East. Drive about 200 meters to Peller.

PELLER ESTATES WINERY ⓦ

290 John Street East, Niagara-on-the-Lake
Phone: 888-673-5537
Online: www.peller.com

Peller has always done really cool things to celebrate Icewine, including its annual January "Bootcamp for Icewine Bon Vivants" to celebrate Niagara's Icewine Fest, as well as the legendary house-made Icewine marshmallows, which visitors can roast outside over open fires amongst the idyllic snow-covered vines. To up the frozen ante, Peller opened The 10 Below Room in the fall of 2015, an Icewine cave built within a giant walk-in freezer in the cellar. Likely the most unique Icewine experience in Niagara, visitors can take either the "Ultimate 10 Below Experience" to learn (and taste!) all things Icewine, or go for the "Greatest Winery Tour" which visits the vineyard and cellar as well. Be sure to try out the Ice Cuvée, traditional method sparkling wine in both blanc and rosé styles, topped with a dosage of Icewine.

Insiders Tip: In the stunning winery boutique, seek out Peller Estates' "Twittens." Warm mittens with removable thumbs — perfect for tweeting your Niagara adventures!

> Take a right on John Street East, then right onto Niagara Parkway. Continue 1 km. Reif will be on your right.

REIF ESTATE WINERY ⓦ

15608 Niagara Parkway, Niagara-on-the-Lake
Phone: 905-468-7738
Online: www.reifwinery.com

Reif began life as a vineyard in the 1970s, supplying grapes for other wineries, then made the switch to a full-fledged winery in 1982. German in heritage, still evident in the building's facade and typography, founder Ewald Reif concentrated on Germanic Rieslings and Icewines. Ewald's nephew Klaus joined in 1987, and shortly after, winemaker Roberto Di-Domenco came on board and began crafting full and rich Bordeaux varietals, including Reif's top-tier First Growth series, only made in best vintages. Try them for yourself at Reif's "best kept secret" sensory bar, offering a selection of tastings, including blind wine tastings in black glasses.

Insider's Tip: As a leading Icewine producer, Reif offers a large library of older vintages for sale. At the time of this writing, the 2003 and 2005 Icewines are available, but if you are interested in a specific vintage, inquire at the tasting bar.

> **Turn right on Niagara Parkway, turn right at Line 3, Inniskillin is on the corner of Line 3 and Niagara Parkway.**

INNISKILLIN

1499 Line 3 Niagara Parkway, Niagara-on-the-Lake
Phone: 888-466-4754
Online: www.inniskillin.com

Inniskillin was one of the first wineries in Niagara, founded in 1975 by Donald Ziraldo and Karl Kaiser, but it wasn't until 1991 that it shot to fame — and brought Ontario along with it — when it famously took top honours at the prestigious Vin Expo in France for its 1989 Vidal Icewine. Fast forward more than 40 years, the winery is still going strong, turning out a wide range of wines, although Icewine is still a feather in the Inniskillin cap. Try the sparkling Cabernet Franc Icewine; its bubbles have the effect of lightening the sweetness. A 1920s-era barn, thought to have been inspired by architect Frank Lloyd Wright, was restored for the winery's use, and has become something of a landmark.

Insider's Tip: Riedel Crystal, the innovative wineglass producer based in Austria, used Inniskillin Icewine to design a glass specifically for Icewine (part of Riedel's Vinum Extreme series).

> **Turn left on Line 3, left onto Concession 2 Road, then right onto York Road. Ravine is on your right.**

RAVINE VINEYARDS

1366 York Road, Niagara-on-the-Lake
Phone: 905-262-8463
Online: www.ravinevineyard.com

Having worked up an appetite, stop at Ravine for a tasting and superb lunch. Known for producing top-notch Burgundy-style Chardonnay and

Bordeaux-style reds, Ravine is an organic winery that sits on 34 bucolic acres in the Niagara sub-appellation of St David's Bench, the warmest area, said to be 20 percent warmer than any other location in the region. The Lowrey family has grown grapes here for 5 generations, dating back to the 1800s, and that pioneering, farm spirit carries over to the charmingly rustic restaurant which bakes its own bread, grows its own vegetables and raises its own pigs. Just this year, the enterprising family began producing dry ciders from locally grown apples and teamed up with a nearby cannery to jar and can their own sauces and produce, so you can purchase components of the dish you enjoyed in the restaurant to take home.

Insider's Tip: Community-focused fun is the name of the game here; visitors can skate on the outdoor rink (flooded by the local fire department, no less) in the winter or try their hand at bocce ball in the summer.

> **Turn right on York Road. Turn right onto Queenston Road, then right onto Concession 5 Road. Coyote's Run is on your right.**

COYOTE'S RUN ⚲

485 Concession 5 Road,. Niagara-on-the-Lake
Phone: 905-682-8310
Online: www.coyotesrunwinery.com

The antithesis of the stately, palatial winery, Coyote's Run is a place where visitors can literally get their boots dirty. It's surrounded by clay – hard, inhospitable, "mean" clay, explains managing partner Jeff Aubry, the kind that Pinot Noir vines just love. Ask nicely, and someone will be happy to show you around the vineyard (weather permitting), where there is a literal divide between red and black clay soils separating the land. The red has a tendency to make more jubilant, soft, red fruit and floral Pinots, while black clay gives Pinots depth, muscle and structure. And yes, coyotes do run here, though they don't really get all that close during the day when the winery is open. Dogs are welcome, as are kids, and there's a bag full of frisbees, soccer balls and horseshoes ready to keep visitors entertained on the back lawn. Casual, down to earth, and friendly, visitors might experience an impromptu jam session coming out of the barrel cellar as winemaker Dave Sheppard and his team have been known to rock out during breaks, or you may be invited into the production area (if it's safe enough) to see what's going on that day.

Insider's Tip: No food facilities on site, though on special days during the warmer months Coyote's Run will feature various local food trucks. Check out the website for exact dates and details..

> **Turn left on Concession 5 Road, right onto Queenston Road, then left onto Concession Road 6. Colaneri is on your right.**

COLANERI ESTATE WINERY ⬤

348 Concession Road 6, Niagara-on-the-Lake
Phone: 905-682-2100
Online: www.colaneriwines.com

Colaneri is a breathtaking winery, an Italian palatial fortress sitting in the centre of 40 acres of vines in the rural setting of the St. David's appellation. As you drive along York Road, the massive building emerges from the flat countryside, intriguing awestruck visitors to imagine what is going on inside. Interestingly, like a grand Italian Cathedral, construction has yet to wrap up despite having opened in 2010, and there's no real end date in sight. However, they probably have the coolest wine boutique and tasting room in Niagara (it will likely move as construction continues) with a large, open balcony of sorts that looks down onto the production area lined with massive stainless steel tanks. As you sample and shop, you can watch cellar hands working away. Opulence and drama aside, the focus here is on family. Each wine is named and labeled after a member of the Colaneris, with the powerful appassimento Bordeaux blend (plus Syrah) representing the whole clan. It's called "Insieme," which means "together" in Italian.

Insider's Tip: Because the building is under ongoing construction, tours aren't offered. However, in the summer you can take a seat on the patio and pretend to be a Marchese with a glass of vino and some antipasto.

> **Turn right on Concession 6 Road, then left onto York Road. Chateau des Charmes is on your right.**

CHÂTEAU DES CHARMES

1025 York Road, Niagara-on- **the-Lake**
Phone: 905-262-4219

Online: www.fromtheboscfamily.com

As you can likely tell from the website address, Château des Charmes is owned and operated by the Bosc family. One of the pioneering wineries of Niagara, Paul Bosc Sr. started the winery almost 40 years ago, believing in the potential of the region for cultivating vinifera vines. Somewhere around 100,000 people visit the winery every year, and from May through October, weekends are filled with weddings on the picturesque estate. Despite the grandness, wines here are astonishingly affordable, among our favourites are a barrel fermented Chardonnay for $14 and spectacular Gamay 'Droit' for $17.

Insider's Tip: If you would like to try something rare and special, pick up a bottle of Eqquuleus, a red Bordeaux blend, its name inspired by Paul Bosc's passion for his Egyptian Arabian horses.

> *Turn left on York Road. Turn left onto Glendale Avenue, left onto Taylor Road, then left again into Niagara College, Continue ahead for 100 meters. Turn left, then right. Benchmark is on your right.*

BENCHMARK RESTAURANT AT NIAGARA COLLEGE

135 Taylor Road, Niagara-on-the-Lake
Phone: 905-641-2252 (ext. 4619)
Online: www.ncbenchmark.ca

Stop for dinner at Benchmark Restaurant, the onsite restaurant for Niagara College's Canadian Food and Wine Institute. Prepared and presented by students, the restaurant's seasonal, rotating menu featured the wines, beer and food created, grown and produced by current students. With numerous awards and accolades, Benchmark's marquee events are often sold out.

Insider's Tip: Reservations are a must, so be sure to call ahead to book.

> *Turn right on Taylor Road; cross over Glendale Avenue. White Oaks is on your right.*

WHITE OAKS CONFERENCE RESORT AND SPA

253 Taylor Road, Niagara-on-the-Lake
Phone: 800-263-5766

Online: www.whiteoaksresort.com

Located just off the highway, this centrally located hotel is a great option — clean and spacious with modern rooms, a first class gym, indoor pool and spa. It's also located right across the street from a new Outlet mall for bargain hunters and shopaholics."

Entry Point:

BUFFALO

WINE TRAILS

DAY TRIP

> *Once over the Peace Bridge, it should take about 40 minutes to reach the Niagara Parkway. Head west on the QEW for about 34 kilometres (21 miles), taking Exit 34 Regional Road 101/Mountain Road. Turn right onto Mountain Road, left onto St. Paul Avenue, then right onto Niagara Town Line, veering left onto Portage Road. At the roundabout take the 2nd exit onto Niagara Parkway.*

THE NIAGARA PARKWAY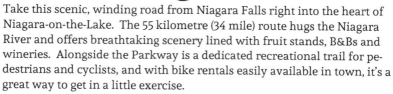

Take this scenic, winding road from Niagara Falls right into the heart of Niagara-on-the-Lake. The 55 kilometre (34 mile) route hugs the Niagara River and offers breathtaking scenery lined with fruit stands, B&Bs and wineries. Alongside the Parkway is a dedicated recreational trail for pedestrians and cyclists, and with bike rentals easily available in town, it's a great way to get in a little exercise.

> *Take a left on Line 3, Inniskillin's driveway is on the left.*

INNISKILLIN

1499 Line 3 Niagara Parkway, Niagara-on-the-Lake
Phone: 888-466-4754
Online: www.inniskillin.com

Inniskillin was one of the first wineries in Niagara, founded in 1975 by Donald Ziraldo and Karl Kaiser, but it wasn't until 1991 that it shot to fame — and brought Ontario along with it — when it famously took top honours at the prestigious Vin Expo in France, for its 1989 Vidal Icewine. Fast forward more than 40 years, the winery is still going strong, turning out a wide range of wines, although Icewine is still a feather in the Inniskillin cap. Try the sparkling Cabernet Franc Icewine; its bubbles have the effect of lightening the sweetness. A 1920s-era barn, thought to have been inspired by architect Frank Lloyd Wright, was restored for the winery's use, and has become something of a landmark.

Insider's Tip: Riedel Crystal, the innovative wineglass producer based in Austria, used Inniskillin Icewine to design a glass specifically for Icewine (part of Riedel's Vinum Extreme series).

> *Turn right on Line 3, then left onto Niagara Parkway; Reif is on the left.*

REIF ESTATE WINERY

15608 Niagara Parkway, Niagara-on-the-Lake
Phone: 905-468-7738
Online: www.reifwinery.com

Reif began life as a vineyard in the 1970s, supplying grapes for other wineries but made the switch to a full-fledged winery in 1982. German in heritage, still evident in the building's facade and typography, founder Ewald Reif concentrated on Germanic Rieslings and Icewines. Ewald's nephew Klaus joined in 1987, and shortly after, winemaker Roberto DiDomenco came on board and started making full and rich Bordeaux varietals, including Reif's top-tier First Growth series, only made in best vintages. Try them for yourself at Reif's "best kept secret" sensory bar, offering a selection of tastings, including blind wine tastings in black glasses.

Insider's Tip: As a leading Icewine producer, Reif offers a large library of older vintages for sale. At the time of this writing, the 2003 and 2005 Icewines are available for purchase, but if you are interested in a specific vintage, inquire at the tasting bar.

> *Take a left on the Niagara Parkway, continue onto Queen's Parade (which turns into Queen). The Exchange Brewery is in town on your right.*

THE EXCHANGE BREWERY

7 Queen Street, Niagara-on-the-Lake
Phone: 905-468-9888
Online: www.exchangebrewery.com

Niagara may be considered wine country, but craft breweries are quickly muscling in on the vinous territory! The latest is the Exchange Brewery, a modern and polished brew house on the main strip of Niagara-on-the-Lake. The refurbished building used to house the area's fist Telephone Exchange, and the brewery subtly nods to the past by serving sample beers on platters that look like old rotary dials and listing beers by number on the menus. With 30 beers available at any given time (8 on tap, 18 in bottle), the focus is on Belgian and sour beers, though a good selection of varying styles is available.

Insider's Tip: There isn't a full menu of food offerings, though simple snacks are available. However, foodies may want to mark Sundays for a visit when hand-rolled sushi is made to order throughout the day.

> **Walk 2 blocks northwest. Treadwell's is on your left.**

TREADWELL FARM-TO-TABLE CUISINE

114 Queen Street, Niagara-on-the-Lake
Phone: 905-934-9797
Online: www.treadwellcuisine.com

We hate to pick favourites in an area as rich in dining as Niagara, but, we always make a point of stopping at Treadwell's for at least one meal when we're in the area, and we have never, ever been disappointed. Located in the heart of Niagara-on-the-Lake, tucked a little back from the street, this quaint bistro owned by father-son team Stephen and James Treadwell, is always buzzing with both locals and tourists in the know. Featuring carefully prepared, but unpretentious, farm to table cuisine and an eclectic, Niagara-focused (what did you expect?) wine list with unique and hard-to-find bottles, the service is friendly, thoughtful and polished. A must visit. n roast outside over open fires amongst the idyllic snow-covered vines.

Insider's Tip: The lobster club, served on duck-fat fried bread with local goat's cheese double smoked bacon, is worth every single calorie.

> **Walk back about a block. Nina's is on your left.**

NINA GELATERIA & PASTRY SHOP

37 Queen Street Niagara-on-the-Lake
Phone: 289-868-8852
Online: www.ninagelateria.com

After lunch, grab an espresso and homemade pastry at Nina's — a great little café on the main strip of NOTL that makes everything in-house and without any artificial ingredients. Recently, the shop added sweet and savoury crepes to the menu which are reportedly moving like ... well, hot crepes. There are a few tables inside the shop, but our choice would be to take a few sweet treats and relax in the nearby park overlooking the water.

Insider's Tip: Whenever we're in town we stock up on the homemade macarons.

> *Head northwest on Queen St., turn left onto Mississauga Rd. (which turns into Niagara Stone Rd.), Trius is on your left.*

TRIUS

1249 Niagara Stone Road, Niagara-on-the-Lake
Phone: 800-582-8412
Online: www.triuswines.com

Trius winemaker Craig McDonald has twice been awarded Winemaker of the Year in the last decade - in 2008 and again last year. The winery focuses on traditional method sparkling wine, and with hundreds of thousands of bottles stacked in the cellar, it's become quite the showpiece on daily tours. Keep an eye out for McDonald's *Showcase* series. Wines in this tier are truly hand crafted in small quantities to reflect the character and personality of each vineyard.

Insider's Tip: McDonald's Bordeaux blend, Trius Red was the only Canadian wine invited to pour at the Oscars.

> *Turn left on Niagara Stone Rd. Hare is on your left.*

THE HARE WINE COMPANY 🍷

769 Niagara Stone Road, Niagara-on-the-Lake
Phone: 905-684-4994
Online: www.theharewineco.com

Having opened late last year, Hare is an impressive addition winery-lined route leading into and out of Niagara-on-the-Lake. Hare focuses on the history of the land and its settlers, and its three wine tiers reflect that in their respective designs, using paper, wood and metal labels. The winery also has a strong focus on entertaining with a heated patio and various events slated throughout the year.

Insider's Tip: Each room is uniquely designed to be its own showpiece: the production area's floor is stained and sealed with Baco Noir grape skins and the barrel cellar is painted to look like guests are tasting in the sky.

> *Turn left on Niagara Stone Road. Southbrook is on your left.*

SOUTHBROOK VINEYARDS 🍷

581 Niagara Stone Road, Niagara-on-the-Lake
Phone: 888-581-1581
Online: www.southbrook.com

With its iconic, long blue wall jutting from the winery, Southbrook is a
beacon on Niagara Stone Road. It was Niagara's first Demeter-certified,
biodynamic winery. It's also organic, and wines are vegetarian and vegan
-friendly. Evidence of the terroir-focused attention is everywhere at this
progressive enterprise. Sheep help maintain the grassy headlands and
fertilize the ground; pigs are raised in a large, enclosed area that straddles
farmland and forest, allowing them to roam far and wide and feast on
acorns. Horse and wagon rides are offered to guests during the warm
months for an insider's view of a working winery-farm. With advanced
booking, visitors can take part in the "Earthly Infused Tasting" pairing
four of Southbrook's wines to four (local and organic) small dishes. If you
show up without a reservation, you can sample local cheeses at the tasting bar for only a few dollars or grab a bite on the patio.

*Insider's Tip: Don't leave without trying Southbrook's Madeira-inspired
fortified wine, "The Anniversary," or the natural Orange Wine, fast becoming the wine world's latest craze.*

> *Turn right on Niagara Stone Road. Turn right onto Concession 7 Road,
left onto Queenston Road, then left onto York Road. Ravine is on your left.*

RAVINE VINEYARDS 🍷 🍴

1366 York Road, Niagara-on-the-Lake
Phone: 905-262-8463
Online: www.ravinevineyard.com

The perfect stop for wine tasting and superb dinner. Known for producing top-notch Burgundy-style Chardonnay and Bordeaux-style reds, Ravine is a biodynamic and certified organic winery that sits on 34 bucolic
acres in the Niagara sub-appellation of St David's Bench, the warmest

area, said to be 20 percent warmer than any other location in the region. The Lowrey family has grown grapes here for 5 generations, dating back to the 1800s, and that pioneering, farm spirit carries over to the charmingly rustic restaurant which bakes its own bread, grows its own vegetables and raises its own pigs, while pairing meals with suggestions by the winemaker. Just this year, the enterprising family started making dry ciders from locally grown apples and teamed up with a nearby cannery to jar and can their own sauces and produce, so you can purchase components of the dish you enjoyed in the restaurant to take home.

Insider's Tip: Community-focused fun is the name of the game here; visitors can skate on the outdoor rink (flooded by the local fire department, no less) in the winter or try their hand at bocce ball in the summer.

> **Turn right on York Road, left onto Glendale Avenue, then right onto Taylor Road. White Oaks is on your right.**

WHITE OAKS CONFERENCE RESORT AND SPA

253 Taylor Road, Niagara-on-the-Lake
Phone: 800-263-5766
Online: www.whiteoaksresort.com

Located just off the highway, this centrally located hotel is a great option — clean and spacious with modern rooms, a first class gym, indoor pool and spa. It's also located right across the street from a new Outlet mall for bargain hunters and shopaholics.

Notes

Entry Point:

BUFFALO

WINE TRAILS

WEEKEND TOUR

Friday

> *Once over the Peace Bridge, it should take about 25 minutes to get to Tide & Vine. Head west on the QEW for about 34 kilometres (21 miles), taking Exit 32 for Thorold Stone Road towards Thorold. Turn right onto Thorold Stone Road. Turn left onto Dorchester Road, right onto O'Neil Street, then right again onto Portage Road. The restaurant is on your right.*

TIDE AND VINE OYSTER HOUSE

3491 Portage Road, Niagara Falls
Phone: 905-356-5782
Online: www.tideandvine.com

Originally one of the most popular food trucks in the Niagara region catering to a number of wineries, farmers markets and festivals, Mike Langley (renowned Oyster Shucker) and partner Kat Steeves established this brick-and-mortar, rustic-modern oyster bar in a Niagara Falls strip mall about a year ago. Choose from a seafood-focused menu (don't miss Kat's Clam Chowder) with a pairing from the curated selection of craft brews and local wines.

Insider's Tip: Reserve in advance and ask for a seat at the bar; chat with the friendly staff and watch the pros shuck at inspiring speed.

> *Turn left on Portage Road and continue onto St. Paul Avenue. Continue onto Four Mile Creek Road. Turn right onto York Road, left onto Concession 2 Road, then right onto East and West Line. Turn left onto Niagara Street and make a slight right onto Rye Street. Turn left onto Cottage Street, right onto King Street, then right onto Picton Street. The hotel is on your right.*

PRINCE OF WALES HOTEL

6 Picton Street, Niagara-on-the-Lake
Phone: 888-669-5566
Online: www.vintage-hotels.com

A landmark hotel that takes up nearly a block on the main strip of Niagara-on-the-Lake, the 150-year-old Victorian structure underwent a full restoration in 1998 to re-create its original charm. Traditional rooms, some of which are pet friendly, will make you feel like you stepped back in time.

Insider's Tip: *If you plan to arrive in the afternoon, treat yourself to High Tea in the Drawing Room (reservations required).*

> *Take a left on Queen Street. Ghost Walk is about 2 blocks on the left.*

GHOST WALK TOURS 🔭

126 Queen Street, Niagara-on-the-Lake
Phone: 855-844-6787
Online: www.ghostwalks.com

Niagara-on-the-Lake is said to be Canada's most haunted town, with many of the historic buildings still housing a spirit or two. Even supernatural skeptics can enjoy the after-dark stroll if for nothing more than the fascinating history of NOTL and the legends that come along with it.

Insider's Tip: Tours run nightly during peak season, but slow down to weekends only during the off-season.

Saturday

PRINCE OF WALES HOTEL 🍴

6 Picton Street, Niagara-on-the-Lake
Phone: 888-669-5566
Online: www.vintage-hotels.com

Enjoy breakfast in the elegant Escabeche dining room, overlooking picturesque Simcoe Park, before checking out and beginning your first day in wine country.

> *Turn left on Queen Street, then left onto Mississauga Street. Continue onto Niagara Stone Road. Jackson-Triggs is on your left.*

JACKSON-TRIGGS 🍷

2145 Niagara Stone Road, Niagara-on-the-Lake
Phone: 905-468-4637
Online: www.jacksontriggswinery.com

Founded by Allan Jackson and Don Triggs back in 1993, the winery has since been acquired by beverage giant Constellation Brands. However, welcoming hospitality and customer-focused enthusiasm still brims at the modern winery. Perhaps the best time to visit is in summer, when the winery hosts its outdoor concert series at the vineyard amphitheatre with music and wine under the stars.

Insider's Tip: In 2016 the winery came out with a new, small production label called "Arterra." Currently only producing 500 cases, there is a Chardonnay, sourced from some of Niagara's best vineyards, and a Pinot Noir, made partially in the appasimento style.

> **Turn left on Niagara Stone Road. Stratus is next door on the left.**

STRATUS

2059 Niagara Stone Road, Niagara-on-the-Lake
Phone: 905-468-1806
Online: www.stratuswines.com

Sleek and urban, Stratus offers a bit of cosmopolitan style to the otherwise pretty and charming winery-lined strip that leads visitors into downtown Niagara-on-the-Lake. LEED-certified, Stratus is one of the world's leading sustainable wineries and an attraction for both architectural and wine lovers alike. The flagship wines are simply called, "Red," and "White," blends of several different varietals that vary in percentage from year to year. Bordeaux-trained Jean-Laurent Groux, who's been making wine in Ontario for 25 years, also successfully pushes boundaries with single varietal Niagara oddballs like Tannat, Sangiovese and Tempranillo, among others.

Insider's Tip: Exceptional, small production Rieslings of long-time employee-turned-garagiste winemaker Charles Baker are attracting global attention.

> **Turn left on Niagara Stone Road. Oast House is on the left.**

OAST HOUSE BREWERS

2017 Niagara Stone Road, Niagara-on-the-Lake
Phone: 289-868-9627
Online: www.oasthousebrewers.com

There's an old proverb that says it takes a lot of great beer to make great wine, and we suggest it takes a great beer (or two) to keep drinking great wine. Stop off at the notable red barn that houses Oast for a refreshing pick-me-up. Having housed everything from a tractor dealership to a radio station, Oast moved into this space in 2012. A true craft brewery, most of the beers take a nod from traditional European styles.

Insider's Tip: The brewery features various chef pop-ups, so check the website for details.

> *Turn right on Niagara Stone Road, then left onto Hunter Road. **Big Head** is on your right.*

BIG HEAD

304 Hunter Road, Niagara-on-the-Lake
Phone: 905-468-4321
Online: www.bigheadwines.ca

You can't get much more up-close and personal to a working winery than Big Head. Visitors make their way through the machinery and equipment of a winery's usually-off limits areas to get to the bright red door of the tasting room. Inside, the immaculate, bright, white room — which doubles as the barrel cellar — is set up with a tasting bar for quick sampling and high-top tables for a more intimate one-on-one sommelier-led experience. Big Head is owned and operated by famed Niagara winemaker Andre Lipinski (who has worked and consulted at easily half a dozen wineries across the region) and his family. Son Jakub is head of operations and daughter Kaja manages events and hospitality. A fan of the concentrated appassimento style of wine making, Lipinski's reds and whites are simultaneously concentrated and generous but also focused and elegant.

Insider's Tip: The sommelier-led tastings are blind in an effort to give visitors an unbiased and open minded approach to the wines. It's worth the experience, but in high season it's best to book a week in advance, off season at least a day.

> *Turn right on Hunter Road. Turn left onto Concession 4 Road, right onto East and Wes Line, then left onto Lakeshore Road. Turn left onto Irvine Road. Small Talk is on your right.*

SMALL TALK VINEYARDS 🍷

1242 Irvine Road, Niagara-on-the-Lake
Phone: 905-935-3535
Online: www.smalltalkvineyards.com

Whimsical and laid back, Small Talk may be "boutique," but the winery makes a big splash with a brightly-coloured entrance and energetic hospitality. On land farmed since the 1950s, visitors can get an inside look by jumping on a wagon for a guided tour of the grounds. Small Talk makes white, red and Icewine, but has recently started producing Shiny Apple Cider, crafted from estate-grown fruit.

Insider's Tip: Visitors love Small Talk's range of Icewines – Vidal, Riesling, and Cabernet Sauvignon.

> *Take the QEW towards Toronto, take Exit 49, ON-406/North Service Road, keeping right and following signs for Third Street South. Turn left onto Third Street Louth, then right onto Fourth Avenue. Creekside is on your left.*

CREEKSIDE WINERY 🍷 🍴

2170 Fourth Avenue, Lincoln
Phone: 877-262-9463
Online: www.creeksidewine.com

Relaxed, friendly and "cottage contemporary," Creekside prides itself on being the kind of place where visitors can feel right at home. Wander out to The Deck and grab a casual barbecue lunch from Chef Nathan Young of In the Smoke Catering. Soak in the country scenery or watch cellar hands hard at work creating spicy, Rhone-styled Syrah and crisp Sauvignon Blancs. Winemaker Rob Power likes to consider Creekside the "alternative varietal winery" for its panache at concentrating on wines other than the Ontario darlings of Chard, Cab Franc, Riesling or Pinot Noir, although they do make a bit of those, too.

Insider's Tip: Creekside is dog-friendly so feel free to bring Fido.

Turn left on Fourth Avenue , left onto Jordan Road, then right onto Haynes Street. Turn right onto King Street, left onto Victoria Avenue, then right onto Moyer Road. Vineland is on your left.

VINELAND ESTATES WINERY

3620 Moyer Road, Vineland
Phone: 888-846-3526
Online: www.vineland.com

One of the most beautiful wineries in North America, Vineland Estates dates back to the 1800s when it was a Mennonite farm, and the original structures are still standing. The century barn, fully restored in 1999, houses a wine tasting bar (served in Spiegelau glassware) and retail store under massive wood beams. Known for producing zesty, vibrant Rieslings, other offerings include Sauvignon Blanc, Cabernet Franc, and a signature Meritage.

Insider's Tip: The winery is said to be haunted with the spirit of the farming family's Grandma. We've taken tours there where guests have had odd things happen; ask about these strange occurrences when you visit.

> **Turn left on Moyer Road, then right onto Cherry Avenue. Tawse is on your right.**

TAWSE WINERY

3955 Cherry Avenue, Vineland
Phone: 905-562-9500
Online: www.tawsewinery.ca

Tawse (pronounced like "paws" but with a "T") only opened to the public in 2005, but it quickly shot to fame as one of Ontario's top wineries. Owner Moray Tawse, who also has holdings in Argentina and France, spared no expense to create premium, age-worthy wines that could hold their own against any in the world. In fact, Moray has hosted cellar dinners pitting his Pinots against famed Burgundies in blind tastings. Committed to organic and biodynamic, winemaker Paul Pender focuses on the land, dividing vineyards in blocks to get the true sense of the terroir. There are 65 labels in total, but top wines include Riesling, Cabernet Franc, Pinot

Noir and Chardonnay.

Insider's Tip: If those wine-filled cellar dinners sound like fun, get on the mailing list, they're usually only advertised that way and often sell out in minutes.

> **Turn right on Cherry Avenue, then left onto King Street. Back 10 is on your right.**

BACK 10 CELLARS

4101 King Street, Beamsville
Phone: 905-562-3365
Online: www.back10cellars.com

Owners Andrew and Christina Brooks quit their jobs in 2002 to buy a derelict farmhouse on 10 acres of land with dreams of planting a vineyard and starting a winery. For about five years they grew grapes for Featherstone, and finally produced their own wines in 2012, making only about 1,000 cases. This "super boutique" experience allows for a more personal experience, as guests are greeted like family by Andrew and Christina. With a short amount of notice, you can try your hand in the vineyard, or indulge in the pleasure of a simple picnic lunch.

Insider's Tip: Tastings are education-focused and aimed to be more personal with private seatings, small bites and a dedicated winery staff member to lead you through the flight.

> **Turn right on King Street. Malivoire is on your left.**

MALIVOIRE

4260 King Street, Beamsville
Phone: 866-644-2244
Online: www.malivoire.com

The namesake winery of Martin Malivoire, whose previous career was supervising special effects for Hollywood films, is as focused on environmental sustainability as it is on premium wine. The picturesque winery is covered with native trees and bushes which help attract wildlife to the eco-friendly site. In the summer, take in the natural landscape with a glass of wine and local cheese on the winery's new patio.

Insider's Tip: The largest bottler of Gamay in North America, Malivoire also makes wine for Rennie Estate – vignerons with about 50 acres of prime Bench land vineyards. Look for handcrafted Pinot Noir and Chardonnay and appassimento styled Bordeaux blends for "Super Niagara" wines..

> **Turn left on King Street. Kew is on your left.**

KEW VINEYARDS

4696 King Street, Beamsville
Phone: 905-563-1539
Online: www.kewvineyards.com

Kew sits at the top of a hill on King Street, and its robins-egg blue sign can be missed if you're not careful, so know that this charming winery is across the street from a large auto mall — a bit weird considering the delicate and pretty tasting room and boutique. Housed in a 160-year-old farm house, it's been lovingly restored in modern-country decor, complete with soft-patterned wallpaper, glittering antique chandeliers and farmhouse-chic shelving. The boutique opens onto the 60-acre vineyard, and visitors are welcome to take a glass for a walk amongst the vines. Indeed, visiting Kew seems more like visiting an old friend than touring a winery.

Insider's Tip: Kew helped to develop the world's first appassimento drying chamber, which the winery uses for Cabernet-blend "Solider's Grant."

> **Take the QEW towards Niagara, exit Glendale Avenue South. Turn right onto Taylor Road. White Oaks is on your right.**

WHITE OAKS CONFERENCE RESORT AND SPA

253 Taylor Road, Niagara-on-the-Lake
Phone: 800-263-5766
Online: www.whiteoaksresort.com

Located just off the highway, this centrally located hotel is a great option – clean and spacious with modern rooms, a first class gym, indoor pool and spa. It's also located right across the street from a new Outlet mall for bargain hunters and shopaholics.

Insiders Tip: Professional and accommodating Concierge are happy to arrange a chauffeured wine tour.

> **Turn right on Taylor Road, as it continues into Niagara Stone Road at the lights. Turn right onto Mary Street. Backhouse is on your right.**

BACKHOUSE

242 Mary Street, Niagara-on-the-Lake
Phone: 289-272-1242
Online: www.backhouse.xyz

Set in the unlikely location of a strip mall is where you'll find Niagara's newest, coolest restaurant. With the look of a modern Scandinavian farmhouse, replete with fur throws, wood piles and animal bone centre pieces, Backhouse is at once sleek and comfy, homey yet industrial. Created by husband-and-wife team Bev Hotchkiss and chef Ryan Crawford, the inventive menu focuses on "cool climate cuisine," with most components sourced locally and many from the on-staff farmer. Items are so fresh that offerings change daily depending on what's available and in season at the farm.

Insider's Tip: In true Canadiana fashion, guests are served a complimentary roasted marshmallow at the end of the meal, but if you are part of the last seating, guests are invited to the open kitchen to roast their own.

Sunday

> *Leaving the hotel, turn left on Taylor Road, left onto Glendale Avenue, then right onto York Road. Ravine is on your left.*

RAVINE VINEYARDS

1366 York Road, Niagara-on-the-Lake
Phone: 905-262-8463
Online: www.ravinevineyard.com

Start the day with brunch at Ravine, a farm-to-table winery restaurant that bakes its own bread, grows its own vegetables and raises its own pigs. The winery produces top-notch, Burgundy-style Chardonnay and

Bordeaux-style reds from organic vineyards the Lowrey family has farmed for five generations.

Insider's Tip: Ravine has teamed up with a nearby cannery to jar and can their own sauces and produce so you can purchase components of the dish you enjoyed in the restaurant to take home.

> **Turn right on York Road; Chateau des Charmes is on your left.**

CHÂTEAU DES CHARMES ⏍

1025 York Road, Niagara-on-the-Lake
Phone: 905-262-4219
Online: www.fromtheboscfamily.com

As you can likely tell from the website url, Château des Charmes is owned and operated by the Bosc family. One of the pioneering wineries of Niagara, Paul Bosc Sr. started the winery almost 40 years ago - though it wasn't until 1994 that the grand chateau was built. Romantic and stately, weekends are filled with picturesque outdoor weddings. Tours run daily in English, French and Japanese and showcase the newly expanded barrel cellar which features 16 rare 5,000 litre French oak casks.

Insider's Tip: $1 from each tour is donated to a local charity.

> **Turn left on York Road, right onto Concession 6 Road, Colaneri is on your left.**

COLANERI ESTATE WINERY ⏍

348 Concession Road 6, Niagara-on-the-Lake
Phone: 905-682-2100
Online: www.colaneriwines.com

Colaneri is a breathtaking winery, an Italian palatial fortress sitting in the centre of 40 acres of vines in the rural setting of the St. David's appellation. As you drive along York Road, the massive building emerges from the flat countryside, intriguing awestruck visitors to imagine what is going on inside. Interestingly, like a grand Italian Cathedral, construction has yet to wrap up despite having opened in 2010, and there's no real end date in sight. However, they probably have the coolest wine boutique and tasting room in Niagara (it will likely move as construction continues) with a large, open balcony of sorts that looks down onto the production area lined with massive stainless steel tanks. As you sample and shop, you can watch cellar hands working away. Opulence and drama aside, the focus here is on family. Each wine is named and labeled after a member of the Colaneris, with the powerful appassimento Bordeaux blend (plus Syrah) representing the whole clan. It's called "Insieme," which means "together" in Italian.

Insider's Tip: Because the building is under ongoing construction, tours aren't offered. However, in the summer you can take a seat on the patio and pretend to be a Marchese with a glass of vino and some antipasto..

> **Turn left on Concession 6 Road, right onto Line 5 Road, then another right onto Four Mile Creek Road. Between the Lines is on your left.**

BETWEEN THE LINES

991 Four Mile Creek Road, Niagara-on-the-Lake
Phone: 905-262-0289
Online: www.betweenthelineswinery.com

A red barn houses this small winery, owned by two of Niagara's youngest proprietors, brothers Yannick and Greg Wertsch, the elder having barely cracked 30. Despite their young age, both have been well-educated in the wine business, both formally at university in their native Germany, and by their parents who began growing grapes on the 40-acre property when they moved to Canada in 1998. The brothers decided to continue the family business but took it one step further, buying out their parents and starting a winery. They specialize in Germanic styles of Riesling, Gewürztraminer, Icewine and unique to Ontario, the red grape Lemberger, dark and powerful in taste and structure. It's worth seeking out, but move quickly as it sells out every year.

Insider's Tip: A few years ago the brothers developed an aromatic sparkling wine in a can – the first in North America – which has been selling like crazy. Perfect to tote on one of your winery picnics.

> **Turn right on Four Mile Creek Road, right onto Niagara Stone Road, then another right onto Queen Street. Treadwell's is on your right.**

TREADWELL FARM-TO-TABLE CUISINE

114 Queen Street, Niagara-on-the-Lake
Phone: 905-934-9797
Online: www.treadwellcuisine.com

Having worked up an appetite, make your way back to town for lunch at Treadwell's. Located in the heart of Niagara-on-the-Lake, tucked a bit back from the street, beside the Starbuck's, this quaint bistro, owned by father-son team Stephen and James Treadwell, is always buzzing with both locals and tourists in the know. Featuring carefully prepared, but unpretentious, farm-to-table cuisine and an eclectic, Niagara-focused (what did you expect?) wine list with unique and hard-to-find bottles, the service is friendly, thoughtful and polished. A must visit.

Insider's Tip: The lobster club, served on duck-fat fried bread with local goat cheese double smoked bacon, is worth every single calorie.

NIAGARA-ON-THE-LAKE

Walk off your lunch with a little window shopping along the main street of Niagara-on-the-Lake, considered the prettiest town in Canada. Among the many shops lining the main street, be sure to check out Oliv Tasting Room which features premium olive oils and vinegars. Wine Country Vintners, owned by Andrew Peller, has a wine tasting bar for a quick and convenient sampling of Niagara wines. Gorgeous architecture, serene parks set against the Lake, elegant restaurants and the famous Shaw Festival all make up this charming place, once a British military base for Empire loyalists fleeing the US during the American Revolution.

> **Head southeast on Queen Street towards the clock tower to Picton Road. Continue to Queen's Parade. Turn right onto John Street East. Two Sisters is on your left.**

TWO SISTERS VINEYARDS

240 John Street East, Niagara-on-the-Lake
Phone: 905-468-0592
Online: www.twosistersvineyards.com

Just on the outskirts of town, Two Sisters looks like the country stead of some ancient Ontario nobility instead of a winery. The property (once a fruit orchard) was purchased in 2005 by the Marotta family, and the two sisters who run the winery, Angela and Melissa, opened to the public in 2013. Massive and stately, symmetrical columns and windows decorate the otherwise flat and precise face of the building; the long driveway is flanked by tall statues of soaring eagles. It may look mannered, but the staff oozes hospitality and warmth to everyone who visits this impressive place.

Insider's Tip: Winemaker Adam Pearce works magic with ultra-premium, small lot Bordeaux-styled reds and select white wines.

> *Turn right on John Street East, Peller is next door on your right..*

PELLER ESTATES WINERY

290 John Street East, Niagara-on-the-Lake
Phone: 888-673-5537
Online: www.peller.com

For a finishing touch, end the day with dinner on the patio of Peller Estates. Barrel House Grill, the award-winning winery restaurant, is headed up by Chef Jason Parsons, a local celebrity thanks to his regular appearances on national television. Taking advantage of Peller's premium Icewine production, Chef Parsons weaves the key ingredient into many of the restaurant's ever-changing seasonal offerings.

Insider's Tip: Last fall, Peller opened the 10 Below Room, an Icewine cave built within a giant walk-in freezer in the winery's cellar. Likely the most unique Icewine experience in Niagara, visitors are handed parkas to wear while they sip and learn in the ice-lined cave.

> *Turn right on John Street East, left onto Queen's Parade, right onto Wellington Street, then right onto Byron Street. Queen's Landing is on your left.*

QUEEN'S LANDING

155 Byron Street, Niagara-on-the-Lake
Phone: 905-468-2195
Online: www.vintage-hotels.com

Situated just a few blocks from its sister hotel, Prince of Wales, Queen's Landing houses 142 rooms outfitted in Georgian-era decor. Resembling a mansion more than a hotel, classic design elements include marble floors, stone courtyards and elegant chandeliers. Before turning in for the night, enjoy a glass of wine on the patio overlooking the harbour in summer, or in the handsome, leather-lined bar in winter.

Notes

Entry Point:

TORONTO

WINE TRAILS-ALTERNATE

DAY TRIP

> *From downtown Toronto the drive will take about 90 minutes to 2 hours without traffic. Take the Gardiner Expressway west for about 5 kilometres (3 miles), continuing as it turns into the QEW west. After about 50 km (31 miles), keep left at the fork to stay on the QEW towards Niagara. Continue another 50 km to Exit 38B Glendale Avenue North towards Niagara on the Lake. Turn right on Glendale Avenue, turn right onto York Road, driving another 3 km (2 miles). Château des Charmes is on your right.*

CHÂTEAU DES CHARMES

1025 York Road, Niagara-on-the-Lake
Phone: 905-262-4219
Online: www.fromtheboscfamily.com

As you can likely tell from the website address, Château des Charmes is owned and operated by the Bosc family. One of the pioneering wineries of Niagara, Paul Bosc Sr. started the winery almost 40 years ago, believing in the potential of the region for cultivating vinifera vines. Somewhere around 100,000 people visit the winery every year, and from May through October, weekends are filled with weddings on the picturesque estate. Despite the grandness, wines here are astonishingly affordable; among our favourites are a barrel fermented Chardonnay for $14 and spectacular Gamay 'Droit' for $17. If you would like to try something rare and special, pick up a bottle of Eqquuleus, a red Bordeaux blend, its name inspired by Paul Bosc's passion for his Egyptian Arabians.

Insider's Tip: Château des Charmes excels at romance. Call ahead and order a picnic basket for 2 to enjoy overlooking the vineyard; it comes with a glass of wine each, light lunch and a private table for $95.

> *Turn right on York Road. Ravine is on your left.*

RAVINE VINEYARDS

1366 York Road, Niagara-on-the-Lake
Phone: 905-262-8463
Online: www.ravinevineyard.com

Known for producing top-notch, Burgundy-style Chardonnay and Bordeaux-style reds, Ravine is a biodynamic and certified organic winery that sits on 34 bucolic acres in the Niagara sub-appellation of St. David's Bench, the warmest area, said to be 20 percent warmer than any other location in the region. Grapes were planted on the Lowrey family farm in 1869, making it the first commercial vineyard in the area. The property was purchased by Blair and Norma Jane (Lowrey) Harber and opened as a winery in 2008. The tasting room is located inside the historic, Georgian-style Woodruff House.

Insider's Tip: Community-focused fun is the name of the game here; visitors can skate on the outdoor rink (flooded by the local fire department, no less) in the winter or try their hand at bocce ball in the summer.

> **Turn left on York Road, then turn left onto Four Mile Creek Road. Between The Lines is on your right.**

BETWEEN THE LINES 🍷

991 Four Mile Creek Road, Niagara-on-the-Lake
Phone: 905-262-0289
Online: www.betweenthelineswinery.com

A red barn houses this small and rustic winery, owned by two of Niagara's youngest proprietors, brothers Yannick and Greg Wertsch, the elder having barely cracked 30. Despite their young age, both have been well-educated in the wine business, both formally at university in their native Germany, and by their parents who began growing grapes on the 40-acre property when they moved to Canada in 1998. The brothers decided to continue the family business but took it one step further, buying out their parents and starting a winery. They specialize in Germanic styles of Riesling, Gewürztraminer, Icewine. and unique to Ontario, the red grape Lemberger, dark and powerful in taste and structure. It's worth seeking out, but move quickly as it sells out every year.

Insider's Tip: The brothers recently developed an aromatic sparkling wine in a can – the first in North America – which is receiving a lot of attention in the area. Paqerfect to tote along on a winery picnic.

> **Turn right on Four Mile Creek Road. Turn right onto Line 5 Road, left onto Concession 2 Road, then right onto East and West Line. Turn left onto Niagara Parkway, then left onto John Street. Two Sisters is on your left.**

TWO SISTERS VINEYARDS

240 John Street East, Niagara-on-the-Lake
Phone: 905-468-0592
Online: www.twosistersvineyards.com

Enjoy lunch at one of Niagara's newest and loveliest winery restaurants. Kitchen 76 at Two Sisters Vineyards features cooked-from-scratch Italian fare, true to the proprietors' Italian heritage — a theme that also comes through in the design of the winery. Pulling up to this impressive estate, you'd think it's been here forever, the country stead of some ancient Ontario nobility. However, the property (once a fruit orchard) was only purchased in 2005 by the Marotta family, and the two sisters who run the winery, Angela and Melissa, opened to the public in 2013. Massive and stately, symmetrical columns and windows decorate the otherwise flat and precise face of the building; the long driveway is flanked by tall statues of soaring eagles. However, hospitality and warmth are the name of the game here, as the winery opens itself up to visitors through both its sophisticated tasting room and the charming, elegantly casual restaurant. During your stop, stuff yourself silly on wood fired pizzas, house-made pastas and freshly baked focaccia. Comfy tables for 2 or 4 are available with sweeping views of the vineyard, or in true famiglia style pull up a chair at the heavy wood communal table in the middle of the dining room.

Insider's Tip: Winemaker Adam Pearce works magic with ultra-premium, small lot Bordeaux-styled reds and select white wines. For added convenience, diners can buy bottles of wine to take home directly from the restaurant; accommodating servers will package the bottles and deliver them to your table, and have it added to the bill.

> *Turn right on John Street, left onto Queen's Parade and follow for 5 minutes. This is the main street of Niagara on the Lake.*

NIAGARA-ON-THE-LAKE 🔭

Stretch your legs after lunch. Take in the sights and sounds of picturesque Niagara-on-the-Lake, considered the prettiest town in Canada. Grab a gelato, fudge or espresso from one of the many shops lining the main street. Gorgeous architecture, serene parks set against the Lake, elegant restaurants and the famous Shaw Festival all make up this little town, which was once a British military base for Empire loyalists fleeing the US during the American Revolution.

> *Head west (away from the clock tower) on Queen Street. Turn left onto Mississauga Street, follow as it turns into Niagara Stone Road. Turn right onto Cushman Road, then left onto Dieppe Road. Turn onto the ramp for QEW towards Toronto. Take exit 49 for ON 406/North Service Road; keep right following signs for North Service Rd/Third Street Louth. Turn left onto Third Street Louth, then right onto S Service Road. Turn left onto Seventh Street Louth, then right onto Fourth Avenue. 3th Street is on your left.*

13TH STREET WINERY

1776 Fourth Avenue, St. Catharines
Phone: 905-984-8463
Online: www.13thstreetwinery.com

Somewhat misleadingly, 13th Street is actually on 4th Avenue, having relocated to the "new" location about a decade ago. Nestled behind tree-lined rolling hills, you could almost miss it if you're not paying attention (luckily, signage is quite big and bold for those of us who are occasionally distracted by pretty scenery). 13th Street has a large portfolio, but is arguably best-known for crisp, dry Rieslings, elegant traditional method sparkling, and earthy, spicy Gamay Noir. Winemaker Jean-Pierre Colas also flexes his muscle with the top tier "Essence" series, wines that he makes only in better vintages from top performing grapes – one year it could be Syrah, the next, Cabernet Franc. Grab a glass and relax on the winery's wrap-around patio, or wander the grounds to admire unique sculptures and paintings by local artists. Casual is the word here, so make yourself at home; just remember, the winery is closed Sundays.

Insiders Tip: Don't leave without picking up a selection of homemade butter tarts at the 13th Street Bakery. There's usually an interesting flavour selection, but our favourite is the traditional tart with raisins.

> *Turn left on Fourth Avenue. Creekside is on your left.*

CREEKSIDE WINERY

2170 Fourth Avenue, Lincoln
Phone: 877-262-9463
Online: www.creeksidewine.com

Relaxed, friendly and "cottage contemporary," Creekside prides itself on being the kind of place where visitors can feel right at home. Specializing in spicy, Rhone-styled Syrah and crisp Sauvignon Blancs, winemaker Rob Power likes to consider Creekside the "alternative varietal winery" for its concentration on wines other than the Ontario darlings of Chard, Cab Franc, Riesling or Pinot Noir, although they do make a bit of those, too. In the summer, a casual back deck is opened for honest-to-goodness BBQ fare.

Insider's Tip: Creekside is dog-friendly so feel free to bring Fido.

> **Turn left on Fourth Avenue. Turn left onto Jordan Road, then right onto Haynes Street. Turn right onto King Street, then left onto Victoria Avenue. Featherstone is on your right.**

FEATHERSTONE ESTATE WINERY

3678 Victoria Avenue, Vineland
Phone: 905-562-1949
Online: www.featherstonewinery.ca

Winemaker David Johnson and Louise Engel bought the property about 15 years ago, setting out to make small-batch, premium wines from grapes grown on their insecticide-free vineyard. There's a focus on working in harmony with nature here; they raise their own pigs and lambs, and the charcuterie is cured in-house. The husband-and-wife team live on the property (the tasting room is a sectioned off portion of the back of their own house), and their dog Bocci is the unofficial greeter (on his Facebook page it says he's the CMO, Chief Mouse Officer). Your dogs are welcome too, as long as they're leashed.

Insider's Tip: Louise is a falconer who flies a bay-winged Harris's Hawk named Amadeus to prevent invading flocks of pest birds from decimating grapes in the vineyard.

> **Turn left on Victoria Avenue, then left onto King Street. Peninsula Ridge is on your left.**

PENINSULA RIDGE

5600 King Street West, Beamsville
Phone: 905-563-0900

Online: www.peninsularidge.com

Relax after a long day and take in a dinner of true farm-to-table cuisine, set in a "Queen Anne Revival" mansion with an outdoor patio for dining during long summer days and nights. Nestled on the site of a 130-year-old farm, Pen Ridge, as it's affectionately known, is the last boutique winery visitors from Toronto will hit on their way back to the city. On a clear day, diners can see the Toronto skyline across the lake from the restaurant in the iconic manor, as seen on Pen Ridge's wine labels. (Dinner is served until 9 PM). The wine boutique is housed in the refurbished wood barn, and has been lovingly restored; when new floor planks needed to be laid down, they sourced wood from old chicken coups of the late 1800s to maintain the integrity of the structure. If you look to the centre of the ceiling, the old hay hook hangs in homage to the barn's previous life. Owner Norm Beal purchased the site in 1999 when it was a fruit orchard. He replanted the spread with grape vines of about eight different varietals, focusing on Chardonnay, Merlot and Syrah, where winemaker Jaime Evans has made his name.

Insider's Tip: The winery produces a fortified wine, or what's known as a mistelle, called Ratafia, which is a distilled plum spirit base with unfermented Chardonnay juice. It's a unique twist on usual wine country offerings.

> **Turn right on King Street, then left onto Main Street. Jordan House is on your right.**

JORDAN HOUSE HOTEL 🛏

3845 Main Street, Jordan
Phone: 800-701-8074
Online: www.innonthetwenty.com

From the same owners as the posh Inn on the Twenty, Jordan House offers a slightly scaled down version in a contemporary, affordable room. Practical, clean and simply stylish, the hotel is also attached to a laid-back tavern which features Niagara wines (of course), plus craft beers and pub grub menu. Weekends showcase local bands.

Insider's Tip: To check in you'll need to visit Inn on the Twenty (5 minutes down the road) as there is no front desk at Jordan House.

Notes

Entry Point:

TORONTO

WINE TRAILS-ALTERNATE

WEEKEND TOUR

Friday

> *From downtown Toronto the drive will take about 90 minutes to 2 hours without traffic. Take the Gardiner Expressway west for about 5 kilometres (3 miles), continuing as it turns into the QEW west. After about 50 km (31 miles), keep left at the fork to stay on the QEW towards Niagara. Continue another 50 km to Exit 38B Glendale Avenue N towards Niagara on the Lake. Turn left on York Road, right onto Airport Road, then another right onto Niagara Stone Road,, continuing onto Mississauga Street. Turn right onto Queen Street, then left onto Gate Street. Oban is on your left.*

OBAN INN

160 Front Street, Niagara-on-the-Lake
Phone: 866-359-6226
Online: www.oban.com

This boutique inn has been transformed in recent years under the capable hands of GM Ian Shulman, who has worked wonders in turning this gorgeous spot into a real destination getaway of catered hospitality. Modern, inviting rooms, an award winning spa, and excellent dining room with friendly staff and a creative kitchen all make for a stay worthy of romantic sojourns and girls' weekends.

Insider's Tip: Take advantage of Oban's excellently priced packages which vary throughout the year, but usually include spa treatments, dinner and a wine tour.

> *Only a leisurely 10 minute walk, stroll along Queen Street to the theatre.*

SHAW FESTIVAL

10 Queen's Parade
Phone: 800-511-7429
Online: www.shawfest.com

Take in a show at the Shaw Festival, the second largest repertory theatre company in North America. Inspired by the works of George Bernard Shaw, the Shaw Festival was founded in the 1960s and has grown to include plays by Shaw's contemporaries as well. Running from April through October each year, the Shaw Festival now takes up four theatres in Niagara on the Lake, the largest being the Festival Theatre on Queen's Parade at the end of the main strip..

Saturday

OBAN INN

160 Front Street, Niagara-on-the-Lake
Phone: 866-359-6226
Online: www.oban.com

Grab a light but satisfying complimentary Continental breakfast, served until 10 AM in the sunroom overlooking English gardens, before checking out and hitting the road for the day.

> *Turn right onto Queen Street, then left onto Mississauga Street which turns into Niagara Stone Road. Jackson Triggs is on your left.*

JACKSON-TRIGGS

2145 Niagara Stone Road, Niagara-on-the-Lake
Phone: 905-468-4637
Online: www.jacksontriggswinery.com

Since its founding in 1993, Jackson-Triggs has become one of Canada's largest wineries, producing well over 100,000 annually. Italian-born winemaker Marco Piccoli, at the helm for the last decade (having previously worked in Italy, Germany and Argentina), focuses on letting the expression of the vineyard show through in each wine. Even though the winery is open all year, perhaps the best time to visit is in the summer, when the winery hosts an outdoor concert series at the vineyard amphitheatre for music and wine under the stars.

Insider's Tip: Pay special attention to "Arterra," the small production label (currently only 500 cases). Chardonnay is sourced from some of Niagara's best vineyards, and Pinot Noir made partially in the appasimento style.

> *Turn left on Niagara Stone Road, turn right onto Hunter Road. Big Head*

is one your right.

BIG HEAD

304 Hunter Road, Niagara-on-the-Lake
Phone: 905-468-4321
Online: www.bigheadwines.ca

You can't get much more up-close and personal to a working winery than Big Head. Visitors make their way through the machinery and equipment of a winery's usually-off limits areas to get to the bright red door of the tasting room. Inside, the immaculate, bright, white room — which doubles as the barrel cellar — is set up with a tasting bar for quick sampling and high-top tables for a more intimate one-on-one sommelier-led experience. Big Head is owned and operated by famed Niagara wine-maker Andre Lipinski (who has worked and consulted at easily half a dozen wineries across the region) and his family. Son Jakub is head of operations and daughter Kaja manages events and hospitality. A fan of the concentrated appassimento style of wine making, Lipinski's reds and whites are simultaneously concentrated and generous but also focused and elegant.

Insider's Tip: The sommelier-led tastings are blind in an effort to give visitors an unbiased and open minded approach to the wines. It's worth the experience, but in high season it's best to book a week in advance, off season at least a day.

> Turn right on Hunter Road, left onto Concession 4 Road; merge right onto Niagara Stone Road. Pilliterri is on your left.

PILLITERRI

1696 Niagara Stone Road, Niagara-on-the-Lake
Phone: 905-468-3147
Online: www.pillitteri.com

Patriarch Gary foresaw where Niagara was headed and converted most of an old fruit farm into vineyards, opening his namesake winery in 1993. Now producing 100,000 cases a year, notably a wide varietal selection of Icewines, the family-owned enterprise attracts thousands of visitors a year and runs three daily tours at 12, 2 and 3 pm.

Insider's Tip: Gary also ran a popular fruit stand when the vineyard was still a fruit farm. That stand still operates in the winery's east wing..

> **Turn right on Niagara Stone Road. Trius is on your left.**

TRIUS

1249 Niagara Stone Road, Niagara-on-the-Lake
Phone: 800-582-8412
Online: www.triuswines.com

Stop here for lunch and choose from a locally-sourced menu against the backdrop of lush vineyards. If it's a nice day, ask for a seat on the patio, and if not, the restaurant's floor-to-ceiling windows will make you feel like you're outside anyway. Trius at Hillebrand was named "Winery of the Year" at InterVin last year (full disclosure: we're both judges for the blind-wine competition), and while it makes a large range of just about every wine Ontario produces, the focus is on sparkling — so much so that the underground sparkling cellar and the winery's spectacular year-round restaurant have been redesigned to showcase the award-winning bubbly. The cellar, which houses nearly half a million bottles of Brut and Brut Rosé, is a featured stop on the tour and the sheer volume always impresses visitors. Tours run daily every 30 minutes, for $15 a person.

Insider's Tip: While you can't go wrong picking up a bottle of bubbly, don't miss winemaker Craig McDonald's sensational Red Shale Vineyard Cabernet Franc.

> **Turn left on Niagara Stone Road, right onto Niagara Regional Road 81, then left onto Welland Canals Parkway, Turn right onto Glendale Avenue, then left onto Pelham Road. Henry of Pelham is on your right.**

HENRY OF PELHAM WINERY FAMILY ESTATE

1469 Pelham Road, St. Catharines
Phone: 905-684-8423
Online: www.henryofpelham.com

Henry of Pelham has one of the most engaging stories of tragedy and triumph in Niagara. It was started in the 80s by Paul Speck Sr., who recruited his three teenaged sons to work weekends, doing everything from planting vines to mopping floors. As the winery began to take off, Paul Sr. passed away, leaving the fledgling winery to the boys, then in their early twenties and teen years. Fast forward 30 years and Henry of Pelham is still family owned and operated by Paul, Matthew and Daniel Speck, who have grown it to a large boutique winery, making somewhere in the ballpark of 100,000 cases a year of premium VQA wines, exported around the world. Despite their success, the winery hasn't lost its welcoming, homey feel; three charmingly rustic buildings sit on the property, the tasting room and boutique, a seasonal restaurant, and a magnificent underground barrel cellar, which runs a story deep and is carved out of the exposed limestone and lined with towering rows of hundreds of barrels.

Insider's Tip: Henry of Pelham has the best Baco Noir in the province (reminiscent of a wine from the northern Rhone); and don't miss the traditional method sparkling, Cuvée Catharine Brut Rosé.

> **Turn left onto Pelham Roasd, turn left onto Fifth Street Louth. Turn left onto King Street, then right onto Jordan Road. Honsberger is on your left.**

HONSBERGER ESTATE ⊌

4060 Jordan Road, Jordan
Phone: 905-562-4339
Online: www.honsbergerestate.com

Driving up the narrow, gravel path to the winery, visitors are greeted with a hand painted sign reading, "welcome to our farm" leaning up against a towering, moss-covered tree. A few feet beyond, is the oh-so-charming grey and red winery and restaurant, fabulously adorned in country chic string lights over the patio and another hand painted, wooden sign pointing the way to the tasting room. You just can't help but smile when you see it. Honsberger has been in the family since the 1800's and has always been a working farm — though only a winery for the last six or so. Brides and grooms have been flocking to this romantic farm setting to celebrate their nuptials in casual, wine country style for years — and previously brought their own wine for the reception until finally the Honsbergers began using some of their acreage to plant Cabernet Franc and Riesling, reaping a two-barrel, boon harvest in 2012. They then brought in winemaker Kelly Mason, who trained under Niagara winemaking great Thomas Bachelder (and still also acts as his Associate wine maker at Domaine Quelyus), and made 200 cases. Kelly has now increased production to

800 cases, still very boutique, which fans snap up by the end of summer.

Insiders Tip: Honsberger's onsite, warm weather, seasonal bistro has people lined up for the wood-oven pizzas. It's seen such success, the winery has built an indoor restaurant for cooler days. Check the website for details and hours.

> *Turn right onto Jordan Road, then right onto Fourth Avenue. Turn left onto Nineteenth Street, right onto Wismer Street, then left onto Main Street. Cave Spring is on your right.*

CAVE SPRING 🍷

3836 Main Street, Lincoln
Phone: 905-562-3581
Online: cavespring.ca

Cave Spring is arguably the most famous producer of Riesling in Niagara with its portfolio ranging from dry to sweet Late Harvest and Icewine. The 30-year-old winery also makes very good, well priced reds and other white varietals. The exceptional restaurant, On the Twenty is next to Cave Spring's tasting room in Jordan Village, while Inn on the Twenty, a charming, 24-suite boutique hotel is across the street.

Insiders Tip: Don't miss the "CSV" Riesling, a terroir-driven wine hand-crafted from Cave Spring's oldest vines.

> *Inn on the Twenty is across the street.*

INN ON THE TWENTY 🛏

3845 Main Street, Jordan
Phone: 800-701-8074
Online: www.innonthetwenty.com

Check in at Inn on the Twenty to freshen up for dinner. The Inn is a charming, 24-suite boutique hotel in the heart of Jordan Village. A tasteful mix of antique and contemporary decor fill the serene, well-serviced Inn. An adjoining spa makes this an ideal spot for romantic getaways; indeed there's a good chance you may see a bride or two roaming the hallways. Free wi-fi, parking, and dog-friendly suites are available.

Insider's Tip: Traveling with a larger group? Check out the Wine Maker's Cottage or Vintage House.

> **From the back of the parking lot, turn right onto Nineteenth Street, then right onto King Street. Turn left onto Victoria Avenue, then right onto Moyer Avenue. Vineland is on your left.**

VINELAND ESTATES WINERY

3620 Moyer Road, Vineland
Phone: 888-846-3526
Online: www.vineland.com

Plan a leisurely dinner at Vineland Estates on your final stop of the day. The winery restaurant was one of the first in Niagara and voted one of the Top 100 restaurants in Canada. The property dates back to the 1800s when it was a Mennonite farm, and the original structures are still standing. The dining room is located in the farmhouse and the stunning boutique and tasting room are housed in a barn with massive wood beams, fully restored in 1999. Known for producing zesty, vibrant Rieslings, enjoy a glass with the cuisine of Chef Justin Downes.

Insider's Tip: The winery is said to be haunted with the spirit of the farming family's Grandma. We've taken tours there where guests have had odd things happen; ask about these strange occurrences when you visit.

Sunday

> **Turn left onto Main Street. Turn right onto King Street, following for about 11 kms (7 miles), August is on your left.**

AUGUST

5204 King Street, Beamsville
Phone: 905-563-0200
Online: www.augustrestaurant.ca

August's Sunday Brunch is legendary. Both locals and in-the-know visitors flock to this place for its huge portions of comfort foods. A popular spot with the nearby wineries, it's not uncommon to rub elbows with wine makers and winery owners over French toast.

Insider's Tip: John Catucci from You Gotta Eat Here *featured the restaurant on his show in 2015 where he feasted on French Toast, Crab Cake Benedict and their Niagara-famous Reuben sandwich.*

> *Turn right onto King Street. KEW is on your right.*

KEW VINEYARDS

4696 King Street, Beamsville
Phone: 905-563-1539
Online: www.kewvineyards.com

Kew sits at the top of a hill on King Street, and its robins-egg blue sign can be missed if you're not careful, so know that this charming winery is across the street from a large auto mall — weird considering the delicate and pretty tasting room and boutique. Housed in a 160-year-old farm house, it's been lovingly restored in modern-country decor, complete with soft-patterned wallpaper, glittering antique chandeliers and farmhouse-chic shelving. The boutique opens onto the 60-acre vineyard, and visitors are welcome to take a glass for a walk amongst the vines. Indeed, visiting Kew seems more like visiting an old friend than touring a winery.

Insider's Tip: Kew helped to develop the world's first appassimento drying chamber, which the winery uses for Cabernet-blend "Solider's Grant." added.

> *Turn right onto King Street. Malivoire is on your right.*

MALIVOIRE

4260 King Street, Beamsville
Phone: 866-644-2244
Online: www.malivoire.com

The namesake winery of Martin Malivoire, whose previous career was making special effects for blockbuster Hollywood films, is as focused on environmental sustainability as it is premium wine. The picturesque winery is covered with native trees and bushes which help attract wildlife to the eco-friendly site. In the summer, take in the natural landscape with a glass of wine and local cheese on the winery's new patio.

Insider's Tip: Malivoire, the largest bottler of Gamay in North America, also makes wine for Rennie Estate, vignerons with about 50 acres of prime Bench land vineyards. Pay special attention to handcrafted Pinot Noir and Chardonnay and appassimento styled Bordeaux blends for "Super Niagara" wines.

> **Turn right onto King Street, left onto Nineteenth Street, then right onto Fourth Avenue. 13th Street is on your right.**

13TH STREET WINERY 🍷

1776 Fourth Avenue, St. Catharines
Phone: 905-984-8463
Online: www.13thstreetwinery.com

Somewhat misleadingly, 13th Street is actually on 4th Avenue, having relocated to the "new" location about a decade ago. Nestled behind tree-lined rolling hills, you could almost miss it if you're not paying attention (luckily signage is quite big and bold for those of us who are occasionally distracted by pretty scenery). The winery has a large portfolio, but is arguably best-known for crisp, dry Rieslings, elegant traditional method sparkling, and earthy, spicy Gamay Noir. Winemaker Jean-Pierre Colas also flexes his muscle with the top-tier "Essence" series, wines that he makes only in better vintages from top performing grapes — one year it could be Syrah, the next Cabernet Franc. Grab a glass and relax on the winery's wrap-around patio, or wander the grounds to admire unique sculptures and paintings by local artists. Casual is the word here, so make yourself at home.

Insiders Tip: Don't leave without picking up a selection of homemade butter tarts at the 13th Street Bakery. There's usually an interesting flavour selection, but our favourite is the traditional tart with raisins..

> **Turn left onto Fourth Avenue. Creekside is on your left.**

CREEKSIDE WINERY 🍷

2170 Fourth Avenue, Lincoln
Phone: 877-262-9463
Online: www.creeksidewine.com

Relaxed, friendly and "cottage contemporary," Creekside prides itself on being the kind of place where visitors can feel right at home. Specializing in spicy, Rhone-styled Syrah and crisp Sauvignon Blancs, winemaker Rob Power likes to consider Creekside the "alternative varietal winery" for its concentration on wines other than the Ontario darlings of Chard, Cab Franc, Riesling or Pinot Noir, although they do make a bit of those, too. In the summer, a casual back deck is opened for honest-to-goodness BBQ fare.

Insider's Tip: Creekside is dog-friendly so feel free to bring Fido..

> *Turn left onto Fourth Ave., turn left onto Seventh Street Louth, getting onto the QEW towards Niagara. Take exit 38B Glendale Ave N toward Niagara-on-the-Lake. Turn right on Glendale Ave., turn right on York Rd., Château des Charmes is on your right.*

CHÂTEAU DES CHARMES 🍷

1025 York Road, Niagara-on-the-Lake
Phone: 905-262-4219
Online: www.fromtheboscfamily.com

As you can likely tell from the website address, Château des Charmes is owned and operated by the Bosc family. One of the pioneering wineries of Niagara, Paul Bosc Sr. started the winery almost 40 years ago, believing in the potential of the region for cultivating vinifera vines. Somewhere around 100,000 people visit the winery every year, and from May through October, weekends are filled with weddings on the picturesque estate. Despite the grandness, wines here are astonishingly affordable, among our favourites are a barrel fermented Chardonnay for $14 and spectacular Gamay 'Droit' for $17.

Insider's Tip: If you would like to try something rare and special, pick up a bottle of Eqquuleus, a red Bordeaux blend, its name inspired by Paul Bosc's passion for his Egyptian Arabian horses.

> *Turn right onto York Road. Ravine is on your left*

RAVINE VINEYARDS 🍷

1366 York Road, Niagara-on-the-Lake
Phone: 905-262-8463
Online: www.ravinevineyard.com

Known for producing top-notch, Burgundy-style Chardonnay and Bordeaux-style reds, Ravine is a biodynamic and certified organic winery that sits on 34 bucolic acres in the Niagara sub-appellation of St. David's Bench, the warmest area, said to be 20 percent warmer than any other location in the region. Grapes were planted on the Lowrey family farm in 1869, making it the first commercial vineyard in the area. The property was purchased by Blair and Norma Jane (Lowrey) Harber and opened as a winery in 2008. The tasting room is located inside the historic, Georgian-style Woodruff House.

Insider's Tip: Community-focused fun is the name of the game here; visitors can skate on the outdoor rink (flooded by the local fire department, no less) in the winter or try their hand at bocce ball in the summer.

> *Turn left onto Four Mile Creek Road, then right onto Niagara Stone Road. Oast is on your right.*

OAST HOUSE BREWERS 🍺

2017 Niagara Stone Road, Niagara-on-the-Lake
Phone: 289-868-9627
Online: www.oasthousebewers.com

There's an old proverb that says it takes a lot of great beer to make great wine, and we suggest it takes a great beer (or two) to keep drinking great wine. Stop off at the notable red barn that houses Oast for a refreshing pick-me-up. Having housed everything from a tractor dealership to a radio station, Oast moved into this space in 2012. A true craft brewery, most of the beers take a nod from traditional European styles.

Insider's Tip: The brewery features various chef pop ups, so check the website for details.

> *Turn right onto Niagara Stone Road. Garrison House is on your left.*

THE GARRISON HOUSE

111C, Unit 2 Garrison Village Drive, Niagara-on-the-Lake
Phone: 905-468-4000
Online: www.thegarrisonhouse.ca
Directly across the street from Jackson-Triggs winery, the Garrison
Houseis a casual gastro-pub, known for burgers made with locally-
sourced beef. The wine list is heavy on Niagara, of course, with a small
selection of international offerings.

Insider's Tip: No reservations here. First come, first served.

> *Turn left onto Niagara Stone Road, then right onto John Street. Pillar and*
Post is on your left.

PILLAR AND POST INN

48 John Street West, Niagara-on-the-Lake
Phone: 905-468-2123
Online: www.vintage-hotels.com

If you're hankering for a little more supernatural phenomenon — or just
like the idea of stepping back in time — turn in at the Pillar and Post Inn,
where as some locals suggest, inexplicable occurrences sometimes happen (included in the book, *Ghosts of Niagara-on-the-Lake*). Originally a
cannery built in the 1800s, the stately, yet welcoming hotel features 122
rooms decorated in modern country chic, complete with exposed beams
and bricks.

Insider's Tip: Have some fun. Play a game of stare-eyes with the portrait
of Lt.-Col. John Butler hanging in the lounge.

Notes

Entry Point:

BUFFALO

WINE TRAILS-ALTERNATE

DAY TRIP

> *Once over the Peace Bridge, it should take about 40 minutes to get to The Foreign Affair Winery. Head west on the QEW for about 56 kilometres (35 miles), taking Exit 57 toward County Rd 24/Victoria Ave. Turn left onto North Service Road. Turn right onto Victoria Avenue, left onto Vadere Ave.nue, left onto Vanguard Road, continuing onto Valentine, then onto Vista Avenue. Foreign Affair is on your right.*

THE FOREIGN AFFAIR WINERY

4890 Victoria Avenue North, Lincoln
Phone: 905-562-9898
Online: www.foreignatfairwinery.com

This winery can be a bit tough to find, tucked in behind the Vineland research centre, but it's worth seeking out. The large moose statue, erected after a long campaign to get it to the winery, should help guide you. Homey and welcoming, this boutique winery takes its inspiration from Italy, and more specifically the appassimento wine making style of Amarone. The enterprise was hatched after founders Len and Marissa Crispino returned from working in Italy where Len served as Ontario trade commissioner. A health scare prompted the couple to follow their dream of opening a winery in 2001 — and in the process, winning an award for innovation from the province. When visiting, ask to hear the Crispino's remarkable and inspiring story.

Insider's Tip: The Crispino's love of both Italy and Canada are captured on the wine labels. All show an Italian countryside, but each wine has a different iconic Canadian animal roaming the Italian backdrop.

> *Turn left on Vista Avenue. Turn left onto Vadere Avenue, right onto Victoria Avenue North, then right onto North Service Road. After 4 kilometres turn right to stay on North Service Road; turn left onto Tufford Road. Dillion's is on your left.*

DILLON'S SMALL BATCH DISTILLERS

4833 Tufford Road, Beamsville
Phone: 905-563-3030
Online: www.dillons.ca

Dillon's is a family owned and operated craft distillery that has taken the spirit world by storm, specializing in gin, white rye, and the currently en vogue Canadian rye whisky, made from "honest ingredients," including fruits, botanicals, and grains sourced locally. Daily tours are available, although hours change depending on the season, so call ahead to ensure your spot.

Insider's Tip: Dillon's produces an exceptional line of bitters that start with Niagara grape distillate to which various fruits, herbs, spices and bittering agents have been added.

> **Turn left on Tufford Road, then right onto King Street (Niagara Regional Road 81). Kew is on your left.**

KEW VINEYARDS

4696 King Street, Beamsville
Phone: 905-563-1539
Online: www.kewvineyards.com

Kew sits at the top of a hill on King Street, and its robins-egg blue sign can be missed if you're not careful, so know that this charming winery is across the street from a large auto mall — weird considering the delicate and pretty tasting room and boutique. Housed in a 160-year-old farm house, it's been lovingly restored in modern-country decor, complete with soft-patterned wallpaper, glittering antique chandeliers and farmhouse-chic shelving. The boutique opens onto the 60-acre vineyard, and visitors are welcome to take a glass for a walk amongst the vines. Indeed, visiting Kew seems more like visiting an old friend than touring a winery.

Insider's Tip: Kew helped to develop the world's first appassimento dry-ing chamber, which the winery uses for Cabernet-blend "Solider's Grant." added.

> **Turn left on King Street. Turn left on Lincoln Avenue, continue onto McLeod Street, then turn left onto Locust Lane, Hidden Bench is on your right.**

HIDDEN BENCH

4152 Locust Lane, Beamsville
Phone: 905-563-8700

Online: www.hiddenbench.com

In 2005, Hidden Bench proprietor (or as he says, vigneron) Howard Thiel left his successful corporate life in Toronto for the greener pastures of Niagara. With a focus on sustainable winemaking to reveal the unique Beamsville Bench terroir, Hidden Bench produces a premium portfolio of Bordeaux-style reds, plus Pinot Noir, Gewurztraminer, Riesling and Fumé Blanc. In the warmer months, Hidden Bench participates in a number of fun festivals and experiences to attract visitors; one that shouldn't be missed is Graze the Bench — a weekend culinary and wine festival featuring five neighbouring wineries which allows guests to wander from location to location, sipping and sampling local wines and food.

Insiders Tip: It's a tough choice to narrow down the splendid wines to one favorite, but don't miss Terrior Cache, an elegant red Bordeaux blend.

> **Turn left on Locust Lane, left onto McLeod Street, then right onto Mountainview Road. Thirty Bench is on your right.**

THIRTY BENCH 🍷

4281 Mountainview Road, Beamsville
Phone: 905-563-1698
Online: www.thirtybench.com

Thirty Bench is a great little winery that specializes in premium Riesling and classic Bordeaux blends. An unassuming wood building which houses the boutique and tasting room belies the power and substance coming from the surrounding vineyard, broken into individual blocks and conveniently used for the winery's top-tier Small Lot series. In 2015, Thirty Bench Emma Garner was named "Winemaker of the Year" at the Ontario Wine Awards. Renovations to the tasting room this year have seen a switch from a standard tasting bar to a seated tasting area where guests can select from either a menu of pre-selected wine flights or build their own. For the more studious, hourly seminars are hosted in a private section to delve deeper into the wines, local terroir, and top grapes.

Insider's Tip: Occasionally back vintages are brought out of the cellar for limited sales, so ask if special bottles might be available for purchase during your visit.

> **Turn right on Mountainview Road, right on King Street, then left on Lincoln Avenue. The Good Earth is on your left.**

THE GOOD EARTH VINEYARD AND WINERY

4556 Lincoln Avenue, Beamsville
Phone: 905-563-6333
Online: www.goodearthfoodandwine.com

This unique wine and culinary destination is the perfect spot for lunch. Founder Nicole Novak opened the quaint bistro in 1998, and has grown it into a beacon for local foodies. The inviting eatery features an ever-changing menu of elegant comfort food and wine country cuisine. Wines are predominantly Chardonnay, Riesling, Pinot Noir and Cabernet Franc from grapes grown in "petite lot" vineyards at the foot of the Beamsville Bench. The Good Earth also has a popular cooking school that offers regular, themed classes throughout the year.

Insider's Tip: While you can certainly try your luck without a reservation, during peak season and on weekends, the bistro is humming, so book in advance.

> **Turn left on Lincoln Avenue. Turn left onto King Street, left onto Seventh Avenue, then right onto Eleventh Street. 16 Mile is on your right.**

16 MILE CELLAR 🍷

3555 Eleventh Street, St. Catherines
Phone: 905-562-5225
Online: www.16milecellar.com

The owner, Toronto attorney Joseph Groia, had been a home-winemaking enthusiast for years before turning his love of the vine into a business in 2010, when he and wife Susan Barnacal purchased 16 Mile. To begin, they employed famed Niagara winemaker Thomas Bachedler as consultant for their Burgundian-influenced Chardonnay and Pinot Noir. Eventually, Regan Kapach came on board as head winemaker. Still very boutique, the small winery produces only 1,000 cases a year.

Insider's Tip: 16 Mile is now open for visits from 11 AM to 4 PM on Saturdays, however, private tours can be arranged by appointment.

> **Turn left on Eleventh Street. Turn right onto King Street, then left onto Seventeenth Street. Westcott Vineyards is on your right.**

WESTCOTT VINEYARDS 🍷

3180 Seventeenth Street, Jordan Station
Phone: 905-562-7517
Online: www.westcottvineyards.com

A truly family owned and operated winery, Grant and Carolyn Westcott opened their name sake winery in 2014 after retiring from corporate life. Daughter Victoria runs the retail side and son Garrett manages the vineyard. Specializing in Chardonnay and Pinot Noir, from which the winery also produces rosé and sparkling, visitors to this elegantly casual winery can order a flight (or just a glass) and chill out on the back deck overlooking the vineyards.

Insider's Tip: Food is provided by Bolete, the St Catharines-based restaurant which has taken Niagara region by storm with its local, well crafted menu.

> ***Turn right on Seventeenth Street, then left onto Eighth Avenue. Eighth turns into Pellham Road. Henry of Pelham is about 5km ahead on your left.***

HENRY OF PELHAM FAMILY ESTATE WINERY

1469 Pelham Road, St. Catharines
Phone: 905-684-8423
Online: www.henryofpelham.com

Henry of Pelham has one of the most engaging stories of tragedy and triumph in Niagara. Started in the 80s by Paul Speck Sr., who recruited his three teenaged sons to work weekends, doing everything from planting vines to mopping floors. As the business began to take off, Paul Sr. passed away, leaving the fledgling winery to the boys, then in their early twenties and teen years. Fast forward 30 years and Henry of Pelham is still family owned and operated by Paul Jr., Matthew and Daniel Speck, who have grown it to a large boutique winery, making somewhere in the ballpark of 100,000 cases a year of premium VQA wines, exported around the world. Despite the success, the winery hasn't lost its welcoming, homey feel; three charmingly rustic buildings sit on the property, the tasting room and boutique, a seasonal restaurant, and a magnificent underground barrel cellar, which runs a story deep and is carved out of the exposed limestone and lined with towering rows of hundreds of barrels.

Insider's Tip: Henry of Pelham has the best Baco Noir in the province (reminiscent of a wine from the northern Rhone); and don't miss the traditional method sparkling, Cuvée Catharine Brut Rosé.

> Turn left on Pelham Road. Turn left onto Fifth Street Louth, then left onto St. Paul Street West. Turn right onto Seventh Street Louth, then left onto Fourth Avenue. 13th Street is on your right.

13TH STREET WINERY ⊕

1776 Fourth Avenue, St. Catharines
Phone: 905-984-8463
Online: www.13thstreetwinery.com

Somewhat misleadingly, 13th Street is actually on 4th Avenue, having relocated to the "new" location about a decade ago. Nestled behind tree-lined rolling hills, you could almost miss it if you're not paying attention (luckily signage is quite big and bold for those of us who are occasionally distracted by pretty scenery). The winery has a large portfolio, but is arguably best-known for crisp, dry Rieslings, elegant traditional method sparkling, and earthy, spicy Gamay Noir. Winemaker Jean-Pierre Colas also flexes his muscle with the top-tier "Essence" series, wines that he makes only in better vintages from top performing grapes — one year it could be Syrah, the next Cabernet Franc. Grab a glass and relax on the winery's wrap-around patio, or wander the grounds to admire unique sculptures and paintings by local artists. Casual is the word here, so make yourself at home.

Insiders Tip: Don't leave without picking up a selection of homemade butter tarts at the 13th Street Bakery. There's usually an interesting flavour selection, but our favourite is the traditional tart with raisins..

> Turn left on Fourth Avenue, right onto Lake Street, then left onto Wellington Street. Wellington Court is on your right.

WELLINGTON COURT ⊘

11 Wellington Street, St. Catharines
Phone: 905-682-5518
Online: www.wellington-court.com

This welcoming, casual-fine dining restaurant in downtown St. Catharines is just minutes from the vineyards of wine country, and its wine list and regionally — inspired menu highlight that proximity. In fact, the restaurant holds weekly staff tastings with local winemakers to select the wines on the list. Started as a café in the 1980s by his mother, chef Erik Peacock inherited the kitchen in the early 90s.

Insider's Tip: Wellington Court also runs Henry of Pelham's seasonal winery restaurant, The Coach House, which runs from May until October.

> Turn right on Wellington Street, right onto Church Street, then left onto Ontario Street. Continue onto Westchester Avenue. Turn right onto Oakdale Avenue, then right onto Merritt Street. Stone Mill in is on your right.

STONE MILL INN

271 Merritt Street, St. Catharines
Phone: 905-680-6455
Online: www.stonemillinn.ca

Built in 1860, the Lybster Mill was one of the pioneering cotton mills in the dominion of Canada. Converted to a luxury boutique hotel about ten years ago, the inn has 34 uniquely decorated rooms, all of which feature stone walls and architectural elements of the original building. The hotel also has an onsite spa and hair salon for visitors looking for a little pampering after a long day.

Notes

Notes

Entry Point:

BUFFALO

WINE TRAILS-ALTERNATE

WEEKEND TOUR

Friday

> *Once over the Peace Bridge, it should take about 30 minutes to get to Trius. Head west on the QEW for about 47 kilometres (29 miles), taking Glendale Avenue towards Niagara-on-the-Lake. Turn right onto Glendale Avenue. Turn left onto York Road, right onto Airport Road, then right onto Niagara Stone Road. Trius is on your right.*

TRIUS

1249 Niagara Stone Road, Niagara-on-the-Lake
Phone: 800-582-8412
Online: www.triuswines.com

Celebrate your arrival in wine country by dining at one of the most romantic restaurant wineries in Niagara-on-the-Lake. Trius has recently been redesigned to showcase their award-winning traditional method sparkling wines, and the airy, light-filled room features views of the sprawling vineyard. Chef Frank Dodd offers a seasonally-based menu that's so local, canola oil is used in place of olive oil. Open year round, with an outdoor patio during the summer months.

Insider's Tip: Before dinner, take in a sparkling wine tour to see the impressive cellar lined with nearly half a million bottles of bubbly!

> *Turn right on Niagara Stone Road, and continue onto Mississauga Street. Turn right onto Queen Street, then left onto Gate Street. Oban is on your left.*

OBAN INN

160 Front Street, Niagara-on-the-Lake
Phone: 866-359-6226
Online: www.oban.com

An historic landmark since 1824, this boutique inn recently fell under the purview of GM Ian Schulman, who has worked wonders in turning this gorgeous spot into a popular destination getaway of catered hospitality.

Insider's Tip: Take advantage of Oban's excellently priced packages which vary throughout the year, but usually include spa treatments, dinner and a wine tour.

OBAN INN

160 Front Street, Niagara-on-the-Lake
Phone: 866-359-6226
Online: www.oban.com

Grab a light but satisfying complimentary Continental breakfast, served until 10 AM in the sunroom overlooking English gardens, before checking out and hitting the road for the day.

> *Turn right on Front Street, and continue onto Ricardo Street. Turn right on Wellington Street, then left onto Queen's Parade. Continue onto Niagara Parkway; turn right onto Line 3 Road. The driveway to Inniskillin is on your left.*

INNISKILLIN

1499 Line 3 Niagara Parkway, Niagara-on-the-Lake
Phone: 888-466-4754
Online: www.inniskillin.com

Inniskillin was one of the first wineries in Niagara, founded in 1975 by Donald Ziraldo and Karl Kaiser, but it wasn't until 1991 that it shot to fame — and brought Ontario along with it — when it famously took top honours at the prestigious Vin Expo in France, for its 1989 Vidal Icewine. Fast forward more than 40 years, the winery is still going strong, turning out a wide range of wines, although Icewine is still a feather in the Inniskillin cap. Try the sparkling Cabernet Franc Icewine; its bubbles have the effect of lightening the sweetness. A 1920s-era barn, thought to have been inspired by architect Frank Lloyd Wright, was restored for the winery's use, and has become something of a landmark.

Insider's Tip: Riedel Crystal, the innovative wineglass producer based in Austria, used Inniskillin Icewine to design a glass specifically for Icewine (part of Riedel's Vinum Extreme series).

> *Turn left on Line 3 Road, right onto Concession 1 Road, then left onto East*

and West Line. Turn left onto Niagara Stone Road. Silvermiith is on your left.

SILVERSMITH BREWING COMPANY 🍺 🍴

1523 Niagara Stone Road, Niagara-on-the-Lake
Phone: 905-468-8447
Online: www.silversmithbrewing.com

Stop for lunch and a pint at Silversmith, a cool little place that you could very easily miss if you didn't know it existed. Housed in an old, vine-covered church that sits between a strip mall and a car dealership, the signage is small, though if you're visiting in summer, you'll see umbrellas on the patio. The slightly incognito location hasn't hurt the craft brewery, as it seems to be pretty full most days, and while we've never visited on a weekend, we're told seats are at a premium by noon. The gastro-pub menu ranges from wings to wursts to po'boy sandwiches, and freshly shucked oysters, and all food items are paired to Silversmith's craft brews.

Insider's Tip: Tours and tastings are available, but like their seats, they are in high demand; booking ahead is a good idea.

> *Pie Plate is across the street..*

PIE PLATE

1516 Niagara Stone Road, Niagara-on-the-Lake
Phone: 905-468-9743
Online: www.thepieplate.com

Recharge with coffee and a baked treat at this Niagara institution. Locals flock here for home-baked pies, obviously, but it's also an off the beaten path destination for thin crust pizzas, unique sandwiches, or savoury meat pies. The small bistro features local wines and craft beers. The menu is constantly changing, so check out their Facebook page for updates.

Insider's Tip: The Pie Plate is located in a converted house and has very subtle signage, so it's easy to miss. It's across from Silversmith Brewing and a car dealership in the enclave of Virgil. Parking is in the back.

> *Turn right on Niagara Stone Road. Hare is on your left.*

THE HARE WINE COMPANY ⊕

769 Niagara Stone Road, Niagara-on-the-Lake
Phone: 905-684-4994
Online: www.theharewineco.com

Near the beginning of Niagara Stone Road, the Hare provides an impressive welcome to the winery-lined route leading into Niagara-on-the-Lake. The winery focuses on the history of the land and its settlers, reflected in three wine tiers with respective designs, using paper, wood and metal labels. Watch for events throughout the year.

Insider's Tip: Each room is uniquely designed to be its own showpiece. The production area floor is stained and sealed with Baco Noir grape skins, and the barrel cellar is painted to appear as though guests are tasting in the sky.

> *Turn left on Niagara Stone Road. Southbrook is on your left.*

SOUTHBROOK VINEYARDS ⊕

581 Niagara Stone Road, Niagara-on-the-Lake
Phone: 888-581-1581
Online: www.southbrook.com

With its iconic, long blue wall jutting from the winery, Southbrook is a beacon on Niagara Stone Road. It was Niagara's first Demeter-certified, biodynamic winery. It's also organic, and wines are vegetarian and vegan-friendly. Evidence of the terroir-focused attention is everywhere at this airy winery. Sheep help maintain the grassy headlands and fertilize the ground; pigs are raised in a large, enclosed area that straddles farmland and forest, allowing them to roam far and wide and feast on acorns. This year, horse and wagon rides are offered to guests during the warm months for an insider's view of a working winery-farm. With advanced booking, visitors can take part in the "Earthly Infused Tasting" pairing four of Southbrook's wines to four (local and organic) small dishes. If you show up without a reservation, you can sample local cheeses at the tasting bar for only a few dollars or grab a bite on the patio.

Insider's Tip: Don't leave without trying Southbrook's Madeira-inspired fortified wine, "The Anniversary," or the natural Orange Wine, fast be-

coming the wine world's latest craze.

> ***Turn left onto Niagara Stone Road; continue past the light onto Taylor Road. NCT is past the mall on your left.***

NIAGARA COLLEGE TEACHING WINERY

135 Taylor Road, Niagara-on-the-Lake
Phone: 905-541-2252 (ext. 4071)
Online: www.niagaracollegewine.ca

Niagara College is the breeding ground for winemakers who go on to work both locally and around the world. Stop by for a tour and tasting of some of the students' award-winning wines. Tours ($10 per person) are educational and in-depth, and can include vineyard walks, facility tours and discussions about Ontario's unique terroir and grape growing.

Insider's Tip: Because this is an opportunity for students to learn by teaching, tours are quite comprehensive, meaning wine lovers get a lot of bang for your buck!

> ***Turn right on Taylor Road, left onto Glendale Road, then left onto Pelham Road. Henry of Pelham is on your right.***

HENRY OF PELHAM FAMILY ESTATE WINERY

1469 Pelham Road, St. Catharines
Phone: 905-684-8423
Online: www.henryofpelham.com

Henry of Pelham has one of the most engaging stories of tragedy and triumph in Niagara. Started in the 80s by Paul Speck Sr., he recruited his three teenaged sons to work weekends, doing everything from planting vines to mopping floors. As the business began to take off, Paul Sr. passed away, leaving the fledgling winery to the boys, then in their early twenties and teen years. Fast forward 30 years and Henry of Pelham is still family owned and operated by Paul Jr., Matthew and Daniel Speck, who have grown it to a large boutique winery, making somewhere in the ballpark of 100,000 cases a year of premium VQA wines, exported around the world. Despite the success, the winery hasn't lost its welcoming, homey feel; three charmingly rustic buildings sit on the property, the tasting room and boutique, a seasonal restaurant, and a magnificent underground barrel cellar, which runs a story deep and is carved out of the exposed limestone and lined with towering rows of hundreds of barrels.

Insider's Tip: Henry of Pelham has the best Baco Noir in the province (reminiscent of a wine from the northern Rhone); and don't miss the traditional method sparkling, Cuvée Catharine Brut Rosé.

> **Turn right on Pelham Road. Continue onto Eighth Avenue, turn right onto Seventeenth Street, then left onto Seventh Avenue. Flat Rock is on your right.**

FLAT ROCK CELLARS 🍷

2727 Seventh Avenue Jordan
Phone: 855-994-8994
Online: www.flatrockcellars.com

Flat Rock only does a handful of wines — Riesling, Pinot Noir, Chardonnay and Pinot-based rosé — but that concentration on a small portfolio allows winemaker Jay Johnston to do those wines really well. Welcoming and hospitable, the hexagon-shaped, environmentally-sustainable building has floor to ceiling glass windows in its boutique, allowing visitors to take in the surrounding vineyards, and, on a clear day, the Toronto skyline from across Lake Ontario.

Insider's Tip: If you call in advance, owner Ed Madronich will personally guide your tour.

> **Turn right on Seventh Avenue, left onto Victoria Avenue, then right onto Sixteenth Road.**

DOMAINE QUEYLUS 🍷

3651 Sixteenth Road, St. Ann
Phone: 855-783-9587
Online: www.queylus.com

Having only been opened a few years, Domaine Queylus is extremely focused on only a few varietals they believe grow best in their vineyards – Cabernet Franc, Merlot, Pinot Noir and Chardonnay. Thomas Bachelder, who also produces premium, terroir-driven Chardonnay and Pinot Noir from Niagara, Oregon, and Burgundy under his own label, is in charge of winemaking which shows through on the elegant, complex and mineral-driven wines.

Insider's Tip: Queylus refers to Gabriel de Queylus, the 17th century French priest who was the first to vinify wild grapes from the shores of Lake Ontario.

> **Turn right on Sixteenth Road. Turn left onto Victoria Avenue, then left onto King Street. Just Cooking is on your right.**

JUST COOKING

3457 King Street, Vineland
Phone: 905-562-3222
Online: www.justcooking.ca

We first heard about this new restaurant after getting enthusiastic recommendations from several local winemakers. This rustic Italian eatery exceeded our own expectations with a superb menu and wine list, both exceptionally well-priced. The unassuming front makes it easy to miss if you don't keep an eye out. Just west of the Victoria Avenue and King Street intersection, Just Cooking features a nearly all VQA wine list and fresh dishes focused on locally-sourced ingredients.

Insider's Tip: While walk-ins are welcome, we strongly recommend reservations; the restaurant is pretty full most days.

> **Turn left on King Street, following for about 3 kns (1.5 miles). Turn left onto Main Street. Inn on the Twenty is on your right.**

INN ON THE TWENTY

3845 Main Street, Jordan
Phone: 800-701-8074
Online: www.innonthetwenty.com

Check in at Inn on the Twenty and freshen up before dinner. The Inn is a charming, 24-suite boutique hotel decorated in a tasteful mix of antique and contemporary furnishings. An adjoining spa makes this an ideal spot for romantic getaways; indeed, there's a good chance you may see a bride or two roaming the hallways. Free wi-fi, parking, and dog friendly suites are available.

Insider's Tip: Traveling with a larger group? Check out the Wine Maker's Cottage or Vintage House.

Sunday

>From the hotel, turn left on Main Street, then right onto King Street. Peninsula Ridge is on your left.

PENINSULA RIDGE 🍷 🍴

5600 King Street West, Beamsville
Phone: 905-563-0900
Online: www.peninsularidge.com

Sitting on the site of a 130-year-old farm, Pen Ridge, as it's affectionately known, is the first boutique winery visitors from Toronto will hit on their way in. An award-winning restaurant takes up the iconic red Victorian house, offering wine country casual elegance with a farm-to-table philosophy. Pull up a seat for the killer brunch.

Insider's Tip: The Grilled Baby Romaine Caesar is the kitchen's twist on a classic. Give it a try.

> Turn left on King Street. Turn left onto Mountainview Road, then left onto Locust Lane. Fielding is on your right.

FIELDING ESTATE WINERY 🍷

4020 Locust Lane, Lincoln
Phone: 888-778-7758
Online: www.fieldingwines.com

A mid-sized boutique winery with a broad range of wines, Fielding is well known for mineral-driven, focused and fresh Pinot Gris and Riesling, and complex, thoughtful Bordeaux blends and Syrahs. Although the wines are serious, don't expect a serious experience — the "mascot" of Fielding is one of the locally-crafted Muskoka chairs, symbolizing their laid-back, relaxed approach. The tasting room is referred to as the "Wine Lodge," and during warm months Fielding puts the emblematic chairs on the winery's deck so visitors can unwind with a glass of wine and take in views of the Lake. On a clear day, you can see the Toronto skyline.

Insider's Tip: Fielding offers a Cheese & Wine Experience from May through October with wines paired to cheese and charcuterie.

> **Turn right on Locust Lane, doubling back past Mike Weir. Hidden Bench is on your left.**

HIDDEN BENCH 🍷

4152 Locust Lane, Beamsville
Phone: 905-563-8700
Online: www.hiddenbench.com

In 2005, Hidden Bench proprietor (or as he says, vigneron) Howard Thiel left his successful corporate life in Toronto for the greener pastures of Niagara. With a focus on sustainable winemaking to reveal the unique Beamsville Bench terroir, Hidden Bench produces a premium portfolio of Bordeaux-style reds, plus Pinot Noir, Gewurtztraminer, Riesling and Fume Blanc. In the warmer months, Hidden Bench participates in a number of fun festivals and experiences to attract visitors; one that shouldn't be missed is Graze the Bench — a weekend culinary and wine festival featuring five neighbouring wineries which allows guests to wander from location to location, sipping and sampling local wines and food.

Insiders Tip: It's a tough choice to narrow down the splendid wines to one favorite, but don't miss Terroir Cache, an elegant red Bordeaux blend.

> **Turn left on Locust Lane, turn left on Mountainview Road. Turn left on Konkle Road, Turn left on Philp Road, turn left on Fly Road, turn left on Cherry Road. Megalo is on your left.**

MEGALOMANIAC WINERY 🍷

3930 Cherry Avenue, Vineland
Phone: 888634-2561
Online: www.megalomaniacwine.com

"Megalo," as industry insiders refer to it, is everything you'd expect from a winery named after ego: opulent, decadent, luxurious and grand. Sitting on the highest point of Vineland surrounded by 96 acres of pristine vineyard, the winery offers spectacular views of the Bench. Despite the majesty, owner John Howard isn't afraid to poke a little fun at his swanky digs: bottle labels feature faceless CEO-types in traditional bowler hats, and each of his nearly 20 or so wines are christened a playful names like, "Narcissist Riesling," "My Way Chardonnay," or "Sparkling Personality" bubbly. Visitors can enjoy them all by the glass on the winery's 7,000 square foot covered patio with cheese and charcuterie.

Insider's Tip: There a serious side to the tongue-in-cheek whimsy - the winery started in 2009 as a fun project to raise funds for the Kids' Health Links Foundation. It saw such success, the winery grew from there, supporting the Foundation to this day.

> **Turn left on Cherry Road, turn left on King St. Redstone is on your right.**

REDSTONE WINERY

4245 King Street, Beamsville
Phone: 844-563-9463
Online: www.redstonewines.ca

Stop at Redstone for lunch. Formerly Thomas and Vaughan Estate Winery, the Lincoln Lakeshore property was purchased in 2009 by Moray Tawse, who named the new winery for its intensely red clay soil and large stones. Redstone's comfortable yet modern bistro features soaring ceilings and wall-to-wall windows to showcase the vineyard backdrop. A perfect setting for the seasonally- and locally-inspired cuisine of Chef David Sider with a glass of organic and biodynamic Merlot, Cabernet Franc, Syrah or Cabernet Sauvignon.

Insider's Tip: The winery just started producing a vibrant, dry cider; you might just take a break from a day of wine tasting.

> **Turn left on King Street. Kacaba is on your right.**

KACABA

3550 King Street, Lincoln
Phone: 866-522-2228
Online: www.kacaba.com

Kacaba offers oodles of charm and serious wine country hospitality. Tours around the tiny winery are for you or your group only. Nothing is off limits and visitors experience a working winery, especially exciting during fall harvest when things are really bustling. Specializing in big, full bodied reds, the Syrahs and Cab Francs are not to be missed.

Insider's Tip: Visitors can try tank samples with discounted "futures" pricing available. When ready, bottles are shipped where applicable, or held indefinitely at the winery for pick-up.

> **> Turn right on King Street, then right onto Victoria Avenue. Featherstone is on your right.**

FEATHERSTONE ESTATE WINERY

3678 Victoria Avenue, Vineland
Phone: 905-562-1949
Online: www.featherstonewinery.ca

Winemaker David Johnson and Louise Engel bought the property about 15 years ago, setting out to make small-batch, premium wines from grapes grown on their insecticide-free vineyard. There's a focus on working in harmony with nature here; they raise their own pigs and lambs, and the charcuterie is cured in-house. The husband-and-wife team live on the property (the tasting room is a sectioned off portion of the back of their own house), and their dog Bocci is the unofficial greeter (on his Facebook page it says he's the CMO, Chief Mouse Officer). Your dogs are welcome too, as long as they're leashed.

Insider's Tip: Louise is a falconer who flies a bay-winged Harris's Hawk named Amadeus to prevent invading flocks of pest birds from decimating grapes in the vineyard.

> **> Turn left on Victoria Avenue, then right onto King Street. Turn left onto Haynes Road, then left onto Jordan Road. Honsberger is on your left.**

HONSBERGER ESTATE

4060 Jordan Road, Jordan
Phone: 905-562-4339
Online: www.honsbergerestate.com

Driving up the narrow, gravel path to the winery, visitors are greeted with a hand painted sign reading, "welcome to our farm" leaning up against a towering, moss-covered tree. A few feet beyond, is the oh-so-charming grey and red winery and restaurant, fabulously adorned in country chic string lights over the patio and another hand painted, wooden sign pointing the way to the tasting room. You just can't help but smile when you see it. Honsberger has been in the family since the 1800's and has always been a working farm - though only a winery for the last six or so. Brides and grooms have been flocking to this romantic farm setting to celebrate their nuptials in casual, wine country style for years - and previously brought their own wine for the reception until finally the Honsbergers began using some of their acreage to plant Cabernet Franc and Riesling, reaping a two-barrel, boon harvest in 2012. They then brought in winemaker Kelly Mason, who trained under Niagara winemaking great Thomas Bachelder (and still also acts as his Associate wine maker at Domaine Quelyus), and made 200 cases. Kelly's now increased production to 800 cases, still very boutique, which fans snap up by the end of summer.

Insider's Tip: Honsberger's onsite, warm weather, seasonal bistro has people lined up for the wood-oven pizzas. It's seen such success, that at the time of this writing, plans for an indoor restaurant are in the works. Check the website for details and hours.

> **Turn right on Jordan Rd., Turn right on Haynes St., turn right on King St., right on Main St. Jordan House is on your right.**

JORDAN HOUSE HOTEL 🛏

3845 Main Street, Jordan Station
Phone: 800-701-8074
Online: www.innonthetwenty.com

Stop here for the night and enjoy a relaxed pub style dinner at the Jordan House Hotel's welcoming tavern. Friendly, laid back and casual, the restaurant features a good selection of local wine and craft beer, and weekends showcase live bands ranging from folk and jazz to rock and country. From the same owners as the posh Inn on the Twenty down the street, this hotel offers a practical, affordable night's stay a clean, contemporary room.

Insider's Tip: To check in you need to visit Inn on the Twenty (5 minutes

Notes

Entry Point:

PRINCE EDWARD COUNTY

WINE TRAILS

DAY TRIP

> *From downtown Toronto, it will take about 2.5 hours without traffic to get to PEC. Head east on the Gardiner Expressway to the Don Valley Parkway North. Take the DVP to the 401 east. Drive along the 401 for about 120 kilometres (75 miles). Take exit 522 Wooler Road/County Road 40 towards Trenton. Turn right onto South Road 40. Turn right onto Loyalist Parkway, continuing about 20 km (12 miles). Turn right onto Greer Road. Rosehall Run is on your left.*

ROSEHALL RUN ⊕

1243 Greer Road, Wellington
Phone: 888-3999-1183
Online: www.rosehallrun.com

Start your day at one of the most well-known and loved wineries in PEC. Dog-friendly and sustainably-farmed, Rosehall Run is a perfect blend of laid back country charm with a modern, forward-thinking focus. Proprietors Lynn Sullivan and winemaker Dan Sullivan were among the first to flock to this burgeoning region, founding the winery in 2001 and opening to the public in 2005. Acclaimed for focused and elegant Pinot Noir and Chardonnay, we're partial to Rosehall's Pinot Gris and Cabernet Franc. On weekends from May through October, the trendy PICNIC food truck is a feature at the winery, where visitors can grab local fare and relax in the picnic area.

Insider's Tip: There's a "secret beach" just up the road from the winery that only locals know about. Get the directions from the winery and stop by for a quick swim or nap on the beach.

> *Casa Dea is next door.*

CASA-DEA ESTATES WINERY ⊕

1186 Greer Road, Wellington
Phone: 613-399-3939
Online: www.casadeaestates.com

Having opened its doors in 2001, Casa-Dea is among the pioneering wineries in the County and also the largest. Of special note, winemaker Paul Battilana's mineral-rich Riesling is made from estate grapes grown in fractured limestone soil. The picturesque winery includes an event space, seasonal restaurant, and bocce ball court. With 65 acres under vine, Casa-Dea invites guests to walk through the vineyards or stroll over to the Love Lock Gate to place a token of your affection.

Insider's Tip: With the ability to host large scale parties, Casa-Dea is a popular spot for weddings.

> **Norman Hardie is across the street.**

NORMAN HARDIE VINEYARD AND WINERY

1152 Greer Road, Wellington
Phone: 613-399-5297
Online: www.normanhardie.com

Norman Hardie is pretty much the rock star winemaker of Prince Edward County. Since starting his eponymous winery in 2003, he has worked tirelessly to promote the region's limestone soils, strikingly similar to the world-famous Burgundy vineyards in France. Originally a sommelier, having earned his accreditation in France, he traveled the world apprenticing as a winemaker before finally settling in PEC. Even though his wines have caught the attention of international wine critics, Norm has earned — and kept — fans for his easy-going approachability and welcoming winery; he even invites guests to help pick grapes in the fall for the harvest. If you're interested in trying your hand at picking, add your name to the mailing list.

Insider's Tip: A few years ago the winery built a wood-fired pizza oven for use in the warm months. It's become so popular they'll pump out 400 handmade pizzas in a day. If you want a seat get there before noon.

> **Turn left on Greer Road, then right onto Loyalist Parkway into Wellington. East & Main is on your left.**

EAST & MAIN

270 Main Street, Wellington
Phone: 613-399-5420
Online: www.eastandmain.ca

Ask any winemaker or winery owner in the County where to eat, and this sleek country bistro is always at the top of their lists. Both charming and polished, the seasonally-inspired menu is described as "luxury comfort food," and could feature anything from house-made charcuterie to locally raised meats and produce — with farm names listed on the menu. A beautiful choice to celebrate a special meal, but don't forget this is wine country, so you can do it in your jeans.

Insider's Tip: At the time of this writing, the restaurant is closed Mondays and Tuesdays, so call ahead for seatings.

> Head west on Main Street. Turn right onto Consecon Street. Turn left onto Danforth Road, right onto Chase Road, then left onto Closson Road. Closson Chase is on the corner.

CLOSSON CHASE

629 Closson Road, Hillier
Phone: 888-201-2300
Online: www.clossonchase.com

Situated at the corner of Closson and Chase Roads, you can't miss the big, purple barn that serves as tasting room and boutique. Concentrating exclusively on Pinot Noir and Chardonnay, the wines are sustainably made, with fruit from both the estate vineyard, and two Niagara vineyards. It's fascinating to taste the same varietals from different vineyards side by side.

Insider's Tip: Keep your eye on the ground if you tour the vineyard; it's full of fragile limestone plates that clearly show fossilized sea life.

> Turn left on Closson Road. The Grange is on your right.

THE GRANGE OF PRINCE EDWARD COUNTY

990 Closson Road, Hillier
Phone: 613-399-1048
Online: www.grangeofprinceedward.com

Recognizing what was happening in Prince Edward County back in the early 2000s, Caroline Granger turned her family farm into a vineyard and winery — and hasn't looked back. With 60 acres under vine, The Grange grows six varietals, and in addition to table wine, produces sparkling and late harvest. Now, with her daughter assisting the winemaking, the mother-daughter duo turn out up to 10,000 cases of 100% estate grown wines every year.

Insider's Tip: To give visitors the full County experience, guests can enjoy a picnic amongst the vines. Baskets include a bottle of wine, locally made offerings and a blanket.

> **Turn right on Closson Road. Hinterland is on your right.**

HINTERLAND

1258 Closson Road, Hillier
Phone: 613-399-2903
Online: www.hinterland.com

The saying, "do one thing and do it well," certainly applies to Hinterland. Since cashing in their day jobs and opening in 2007, partners Vickie Samaras and Jonas Newman have only crafted sparkling wines — and they've become amongst the most sought-after bottles in the province. Hinterland offers five varieties of bubbly, including an "Ancestral" (the original way sparkling was made by French monks in the 1500s), but you'll have to move fast, as fans are quick to snap up the stock.

Insider's Tip: Last year, Hinterland co-founded the County Road Beer Company which opened right next door to the winery.

> **Turn left on Closson Road. Turn right onto Benway Road, left onto Danforth Road, then right onto Consecon Street. Turn left onto Wellington Street, then right onto Wharf Street.**

DRAKE DEVONSHIRE

24 Wharf Street, Wellington
Phone: 613-399-3338
Online: www.drakedevonshire.ca

End your day in true County style at the hippest boutique hotel and restaurant in the region. The country cousin of Toronto's famed Drake Hotel, the Devonshire opened just a few years ago with an urban splash. The barn-like, lake-facing dining room is wall-to-wall windows and regularly features local indie musicians. An excellent, ever-changing menu is focused on farm- and lake-to-table cuisine. When you're ready to hit the hay, the Drake offers 11 guest rooms and 2 suites, (one of which is a double), all uniquely custom designed to reflect the aesthetic of the County.

Insider's Tip: Drake Devonshire is in high demand, so book your stay and dinner reservation well in advance to avoid disappointment. .

Entry Point:

PRINCE EDWARD COUNTY

WINE TRAILS

WEEKEND TOUR

Friday

> *From downtown Toronto, it will take about 2.5 hours without traffic to get to PEC. Head east on the Gardiner Expressway to the Don Valley Parkway North. Take the DVP to the 401 east. Drive along the 401 for about 120 kilometres (75 miles). Take exit 533 Wooler Road/County Road 40 towards Trenton. Turn right onto Wooler Road South. Turn right onto Loyalist Parkway, continuing about 20 km (12 miles). Turn left onto Danforth Road. Hubbs Creek is your right.*

HUBBS CREEK VINEYARD

562 Danforth Road, Wellington
Phone: 647-521-2395
Online: www.hubbscreekvineyard.ca

Kick start your weekend at the family owned and operated winery, Hubbs Creek. The vineyard was planted in 2002, with the first wines released a few years ago to critical acclaim. Focusing on Pinot Noir, Pinot Gris, Chardonnay and a Gamay Rosé, the vineyard is on a 500-million year old geological formation known as the "Lindsay formation." With rich lime content, ideally suited for Burgundian varietals, proprietor/winemaker John Battista Calvieri aims to let that terroir come through in his wines.

Insider's Tip: The winery is open weekends from May to October, with tours by appointment only.

> *Karlo Estates is next door.*

KARLO ESTATES

561 Danforth Road, Wellington
Phone: 613-399-3000
Online: www.karloestates.com

Set in a barn dating back to the 1800s, Karlo Estates is a boutique, artisan winery with a large and diverse portfolio that not only includes the mainstays of Ontario varietals, but also Sangiovese, Petit Verdot and fortified red and white wines. Sherry Karlo and the late Richard Karlo founded the winery in 2005, opened to the public in 2010, and have grown it into a popular destination with private event space, art gallery and North America's largest dry stone bridge. The winery also makes wine for famed NHL player Doug Gilmour.

Insider's Tip: Guests are encouraged to bring a picnic and stroll the vineyards or wander out with a glass of wine to check out the stone bridge.

> Head east on Danforth Road. Turn right onto Consecon Street, left onto Wellington Main Street, then right onto Wharf Street. The Drake is on your right.

DRAKE DEVONSHIRE

24 Wharf Street, Wellington
Phone: 613-399-3338
Online: www.drakedevonshire.ca

This self-described "quirky" boutique hotel has been making headlines since opening in the County in 2014. It's not the cheapest place in town, but its hip-yet-rural appeal keep the rooms and restaurant booked solid most days. The dining room is all windows for uninterrupted views of the Lake, featuring "lake-to-table" cuisine paired with County wines, and suites are appointed in a blend of custom furniture and antiques.

Insider's Tip: A lakeside firepit for sipping wines on the beach after sundown keeps "Camp Drake" guests cozy and happy.

Saturday

DRAKE DEVONSHIRE

24 Wharf Street, Wellington
Phone: 613-399-3338
Online: www.drakedevonshire.ca

Grab a hearty breakfast at the hotel (8:30 to 10:30 AM) before heading out for the day.

> About a 2 minute walk from the hotel, make a left onto Wharf Street, then right onto Main Street.

WELLINGTON FARMERS MARKET 🛒

243 Main Street, Wellington
Online: facebook.com/WellingtonFarmersMarket

This popular outdoor market is a community staple, running Saturdays from May through October. Sample and shop for local produce, baking, meats, preserves, arts and crafts while you meander through the picturesque country town.

> *Head west on Main Street, which turns into Highway 33/Loyalist Parkway.*

SANDBANKS ESTATE WINERY 🍷

17598 Loyalist Parkway, Wellington
Phone: 613-399-1839
Online: www.sandbankswinery.com

One of Prince Edward County's oldest wineries, Sandbanks is not to be missed. Quebec native Catherine Langlois purchased the property in 2001 after falling in love with the area. The winery features regular entertainment, as well as onsite art gallery, and visitors are welcome to relax in the gazebo, tasting Sandbanks large portfolio of award-winning wines. Guided vineyard tours are offered at 10:30 AM and 2 PM (weather permitting).

Insider's Tip: The winery has local cheese and charcuterie available for purchase, or you can bring your own picnic to enjoy in the vineyard.

> *Turn left on Loyalist Parkway. By Chadsey's Cairns is on your left.*

BY CHADSEY'S CAIRNS 🍷

17432 Loyalist Parkway
Phone: 613-399-2992
Online: www.bychadseyscairns.com

The winery's interesting name comes from the original settler who lived on the site 200 years ago. A religious man, Ira Chadsey built stone markers (or cairns) to help guide him home in the afterlife, and they still stand today. Offerings include Ontario stalwarts Chardonnay, Riesling and

Pinot Noir, but also rarer Muscat, Chenin Blanc, and St. Laurent, grown in ancient beach soils that stretch along Lake Ontario.

Insider's Tip: Ask to hear the interesting tale of Ira Chadsey's life and unsolved death, it's a great story to hear over a glass of wine.

> **Turn left on Loyalist Parkway, then left onto Hubbs Creek Road. Keint-he is on your left.**

KEINT-HE WINERY & VINEYARDS

49 Hubbs Creek Road, Wellington
Phone: 613-399-5308
Online: www.keintehe.ca

Pronounced *KENT-hay*, the name is derived from the Seneca aboriginal village, early inhabitants of the area. After retiring from corporate life, proprietor Ron Rogers founded the winery in 2007, specializing in French varietals, including Pinot Noir, Chardonnay, Pinot Gris and Syrah amongst others. Not shy about his efforts to emulate Burgundy, wine-maker Lee Baker's focus is on cool climate, terroir-driven styled wines with lots of mineral notes.

Insider's Tip: The winery uses both County and Niagara fruit; it's fascinating to try varietals from the same vintage but different sites.

> **Turn right on Hubbs Creek Road, right onto Loyalist Parkway, then right onto Station Road. Stanner's is on your right.**

STANNER'S VINEYARD

76 Station Road, Hillier
Phone: 613-661-3361
Online: www.stanersvineyard.ca

One of the newer County wineries, Stanners is owned and operated by Cliff and Dorothy Stanners, along with son and daughter-in-law Colin and Mary. The family's boutique, namesake winery opened in 2010, focusing primarily on Pinot Noir, as well as Pinot Gris, Chardonnay and Cabernet Franc. The operation is small, but very hands on, and well worth a visit.

Insider's Tip: Friendly, small and relaxed, Stanner's offers tours to interested guests, but in keeping with the laid back nature, nothing is too planned (which is very refreshing).

> **Turn left on Station Road, left onto Loyalist Parkway, then right onto Greer Road. Norman Hardie is on your right.**

NORMAN HARDIE VINEYARD AND WINERY

1152 Greer Road, Wellington
Phone: 613-399-5297
Online: www.normanhardie.com

Get here early to ensure a spot on the 60-seat patio. As famous as Norman Hardie is for his wines, it could be argued the winery's become just as famous for its hand-crafted wood oven pizzas. There's generally a line of hungry foodies by noon and Norm says they crank out about 400 pizzas a day. Enjoy your coveted 'za on the outdoor patio overlooking the vineyard with a glass of Norm's mineral-driven Chardonnay or earthy Pinot Noir.

Insider's Tip: Be sure to order a tomato salad from the winery's organic tomato garden. You've never tasted a tomato like it.

> **Rosehall Run is across the street.**

ROSEHALL RUN

1243 Greer Road, Wellington
Phone: 888-3999-1183
Online: www.rosehallrun.com

Dog-friendly and sustainably-farmed, Rosehall Run is a perfect blend of laid-back country charm with a modern, forward-thinking focus. Proprietors Lynn Sullivan and winemaker Dan Sullivan were among the first to flock to this burgeoning region, founding the winery in 2001 and opening to the public in 2005. Acclaimed for focused and elegant Pinot Noir and Chardonnay, we're partial to Rosehall's Pinot Gris and Cabernet Franc. On weekends from May through October, the trendy PICNIC food truck is a feature at the winery, where visitors can grab local fare and relax in the picnic area.

Insider's Tip: There's a "secret beach" just up the road from the winery that only locals know about. Get the directions from the winery and stop by for a quick swim or nap on the beach.

> Turn right on Greer Road. Turn right onto Loyalist Parkway, right onto Bloomfield Main Street, then right onto Stanley Street, following the bends into the park.

SANDBANKS PROVINCIAL PARK 🔭

3004 County Rd. 12 RR#1, Picton
Phone: 613-393-3319
Online: www.ontarioparks.com

Take a break from wining and dining and get in touch with your inner beach bum. Known for its white sands and crystal clear waters this is Canada's answer to the Caribbean. There are three sandy beaches in total, with rolling dunes and hiking trails to cure your wanderlust.

Insider's Tip: Outlet Beach with its shallow waters and gentle drop off is ideal for young families.

> Head east on Lake Shore Lodge Road, keeping to the left for County Road 12. Turn right onto County Road 18, then right onto County Road 10. Turn right onto County Road 24, then left onto Lighthall Road.

LIGHTHALL VINEYARDS 🍷

308 Lighthall Road, Cherry Valley
Phone: 613-767-9155
Online: www.lighthallvineyards.com

Family owned and operated since 2009, Lighthall produces premium estate-grown wines in small quantities. The tasting bar is inside the production area, providing visitors an inside view of the winery. The low production but high quality ratio mean wines sell out very quickly.

Insider's Tip: If proprietor/winemaker Glenn Symons wasn't busy enough, he recently added the title of cheesemaker to his resume. For the last few years he was has been making cheese to pair with his wines for the tasting bar, and now he sells to the public .

> *Head northwest on Lighthall Road. Turn right onto County Road 24, left onto County Road 10, then right to stay on County Road 10. Turn left onto Prince Edward County Road 1; take the roundabout to turn left onto Loyalist Parkway into Bloomfield. Angéline's is on your left.*

ANGÉLINE'S INN 🛏️

433 Main Street, Bloomfield
Phone: 613-393-3301
Online: www.angelines.ca

This eclectic 17-room inn has been operated by the Fida family for nearly 30 years. Innkeeper Alexandre Fida has appointed the rooms with original art and vintage furniture for what he calls his signature "quirky and cozy" style.

Insider's Tip: Angéline's property features suites in a Victorian mansion, but also a contemporary motor inn and three cottages, perfect for larger groups.

THE HUBB EATERY & LOUNGE 🍴

433 Main Street, Bloomfield
Phone: 613-393-3301
Online: www.angelines.ca

Simple, bright and modern, The Hubb at Angéline's features a revolving menu of local options, acclaimed wine list and seasonal cocktails. The creative culinary souls behind this popular eatery are husband and wife team Chef Elliot Reynolds and Sommelier Laura Borutski. After taking over the restaurant a few years ago they implemented their own style, keeping food and drinks casual, unpretentious, and inviting.

Insider's Tip: Hubb fans love the chalkboard options, with most suggesting to eat everything listed.

Sunday

> *Turn left on Bloomfield Main Street. Turn left onto Wellington Loyalist Parkway, becoming Wellington Main Street Tall Poppy is on left.*

TALL POPPY CAFÉ

298 Main Street, Wellington
Phone: 613-399-2233
Online: www.tallpoppycafe.com

Open for breakfast at 7 AM, this welcoming, comfortable café features fresh, wholesome foods that are mostly sourced from their own organic farm. Serving some of the best locally-roasted coffee in the County, Tall Poppy has a dedicated commitment to environment — even offering a discount to patrons who bring their own cups for coffee-to-go.

Insider's Tip: The café also features the works of local artists with collections changing bi-monthly.

> *Turn left onto Loyalist Parkway. Turn right onto Concession Road, then left onto Danforth Road. Turn right onto Chase Road, then left onto Closson Road. Lacey Estates is on your right.*

LACEY ESTATES

804 Closson Road, Hillier
Phone: 613-399-2598
Online: www.laceyestates.com

With production from 100% estate grown grapes, Lacey concentrates on hand-crafted small production wines including Baco Noir, Gewurztraminer and Pinot Gris. Winemaker Kimball Lacey worked his way around the county assisting in winemaking for Norman Hardie and Closson Chase, before he and his family founded the property in 2009.

Insider's Tip: The small and focused winery offers a selection of cheeses from local artisans. Visitors are welcome to enjoy a glass of wine with a cheese plate on the winery's front porch.

> *Turn left on Closson Road. Hinterland is on your right.*

HINTERLAND

1258 Closson Road, Hillier
Phone: 613-399-2903
Online: www.hinterland.com

The saying, "do one thing and do it well," certainly applies to Hinterland. Since cashing in their day jobs and opening in 2007, partners Vickie Samaras and Jonas Newman have only crafted sparkling wines — and they've become amongst the most sought-after bottles in the province. Hinterland offers five varieties of bubbly, including an "Ancestral" (the original way sparkling was made by French monks in the 1500s), but you'll have to move fast as fans are quick to snap up the stock.

Insider's Tip: Last year, Hinterland co-founded the County Road Beer Company which opened next door to the winery.

COUNTY ROAD BEER COMPANY 🍺

1258 Closson Road, Hillier
Phone: 613-399-2903
Online: www.countyrdbeer.com

The newest project of Hinterland's bubble masters Vickie Samaras and Jonas Newman, County Road produces premium beers, including a blonde ale, pale ale, farmhouse saison and American stout. The Tap Room officially opened this past February, offering pints and flights, along with small plates from soup to nuts.

Insider's Tip: Hops are purchased locally when possible, with a batch grown at nearby Pleasant Valley Hops Farm.

› Turn left on Closson Road, doubling back. The Old Third is on the right.

THE OLD THIRD 🍷

251 Closson Road, Hillier
Phone: 613-471-0471
Online: www.theoldthird.com

Even though this is primarily a Pinot Noir winery, The Old Third really popped up on our radar a few years ago when we tasted their spectacular Cabernet Franc. Purchased around 2004 by Bruno Francois and Jens Korberg, the duo takes what they call a "reasoned approach" to organic farming, reducing the use of chemicals for healthier soils. Producing both wine and cider, their pride and joy is the refurbished 1860s barn that was completely restored about 10 years ago and currently houses the winery and tasting room.

Insider's Tip: The Old Third employs a vintages program, pre-selling certain wines in limited quantities before they're released.

> Turn right on Closson Road, left onto County Road 2, then right onto County Road 1, Huff Estates is on your left.

HUFF ESTATES 🍷

2274 County Road #1, Bloomfield
Phone: 866-484-4667
Online: www.huffestates.com

Stop here for lunch, either on the covered patio or window-lined restaurant. Surrounded by gorgeously landscaped property and vineyards, Huff is at once a winery, restaurant, art gallery and modern inn all rolled into one, though people here will tell you that despite state-of-the-art amenities, the focus here has always been on wine. Indeed, this winery has become well known for elegant county favourites Pinot Gris, Pinot Noir and Chardonnay, but also exceptional Gamay and Merlot.

Insider's Tip: Ask for a table on the patio overlooking the vineyard; lunch is prepared by Chef Sebastien Schwab from May through October.

> Turn left on County Road 1, then right onto ON-62 South which takes you into Bloomfield Village.

BLOOMFIELD 🔭 🛒

This quaint, rural village is a highlighted destination point on the County's Taste and Arts Trails for its unique art galleries and studios, exceptional cafés and restaurants, wonderful vegetable stands, eclectic antique shops and gorgeous historic buildings.

Insider's Tip: The quirky antique store, Dead People's Stuff, is a constant draw for serious antiquers and casual shoppers.

> Head northeast along Loyalist Parkway. Barley Days is on your left.

BARLEY DAYS BREWERY 🍺

13730 Loyalist Parkway, Picton
Phone: 613-476-7468
Online: www.barleydaysbrewery.com

Named after the late-1800s heyday, when Prince Edward County barley was in demand around the world as a premium malting grain, this decade-old craft brewery has earned a loyal following of dedicated fans. While head brewer Brett French pushes boundaries with new and exciting beer styles, fresh lagers and ales are a mainstay.

Insider's Tip: While Barley Days beer occasionally comes through the LCBO, it's pretty much only available at the brewery.

> *Turn left on Loyalist Parkway, taking the bend to the left which turns into County Road 49. Blumen Garden Bistro is on your left.*

BLUMEN GARDEN BISTRO 🍴

647 Highway 49, Picton
Phone: 613-476-6841
Online: www.blumengardenbistro.com

For your final stop of the weekend, travel 10 minutes down the road for dinner at one of the most popular restaurants in the County. Located in an idyllic country setting, surrounded by gardens, this charming, polished restaurant has been operating for nearly a decade by Chef/Owner Andreas Feller, incorporating local produce whenever available.

Insider's Tip: Braised rabbit gnocchi is easily the star of the menu; save room for house-made ice cream for dessert.

> *Turn right on Hwy 49, continuing onto Pincton Main Street West. At the roundabout take the first exit onto Prince Edward County Road 1. Huff Estates is on your right.*

HUFF ESTATES WINERY AND INN

2274 County Road #1, Bloomfield
Phone: 866-484-4667
Online: www.huffestates.com

Take a short 15 minute drive back to Huff Estates Inn, a sophisticated and elegant hotel featuring 21 rooms ranging from suites with 2 double beds up to the Winemaker's Suite — an apartment with its own entrance, wrap around patio and 2 baths.

Insider's Tip: Guests are treated to complimentary tasting and tour at the adjacent winery .

Notes

Entry Point:

TORONTO

SCENIC & HISTORIC

DAY TRIP

> *From Toronto, take the Queen Elizabeth Way to exit 55, Jordan Road. Turn left at the stop sign, left onto Jordan Road, then left onto the North Service Road. La Grande Hermine is on the right.*

LA GRANDE HERMINE 👁️

North Service Road, Jordan

Driving along the QEW from Toronto towards Niagara, you'll see the slightly spooky sight of a tilting, semi-beached, abandoned, 140-foot ship. Rusted, neglected and decaying, it isn't able to be boarded, but nonetheless attracts thousands of curious gawkers for a closer view, wondering how it got there in the first place. La Grande Hermine (The Big Weasel) is a replica of the largest ship French explorer Jacques Cartier sailed and was built in 1914. Over its lifetime, it was a ferry, a cargo ship, even a restaurant. It was towed to Jordan Harbour in 1997 as the owner was hoping to get the green light to bring it closer to Niagara Falls and turn it into a gambling boat, but he passed away before the licensing went through. It's been sitting and half-floating in the Harbour ever since. In the early 2000s, it was the victim of an arson fire, further adding to the mystique of the "Pirate Ship of Niagara."

> *Double back to the QEW, keeping right at the fork (follow signs for Niagara Falls), take the exit to the 420, turn left on Clifton Hill, turn right onto Niagara Parkway.*

HORNBLOWER NIAGARA CRUISES 👁️

5920 Niagara Road, Niagara Falls
Phone: 855-264-4227
Online: www.niagaracruises.com

Probably the best tourist experience in Niagara Falls, this exhilarating boat cruise gets you up close — like, really up close — to the thunderous Falls. The 30-minute boat ride takes you past the American Falls and into the heart of the Canadian Falls, otherwise known as Horseshoe Falls.

Insider's Tip: Complimentary, recyclable plastic ponchos are provided, but if you want to get a view of the Falls, and not the backs of heads, you will get wet. It's wise to bring a change of clothes.

CLIFTON HILL

Phone: 905-358-3676
Online: www.clifton.com

A major tourist destination, this strip has all the fun houses, haunted houses, wax museums and novelty museums you could possibly stuff onto one, flashing, neon-lit street. Ferris wheels, glow-in-the-dark bowling, glow-in-the-dark golf, fudge factories and family restaurants all make up the enticing energy of Clifton Hill.

Insider's Tip: Go online to get passes to attractions which are often featured at a discount.

NIAGARA BREWING COMPANY

4915-A Clifton Hill, Niagara Falls
Phone: 905-374-4444
Online: www.niagarabrewingcompany.com

After you've had enough of the bright lights, ringing bells, and whirling sights of Clifton Hill, escape to the Niagara Brewing Company for lunch and some much-needed refreshment. Only steps from the Falls, this craft brewpub opened last year and offers a selection of always-available beers plus a variety of seasonal options. An in-house restaurant, "The Kitchen," serves a range of small bites for snacking, soft pretzels and cheese and charcuterie boards, as well as a selection of hearty sandwiches, crafted specifically to complement the beers.

Insider's Tip: The brewery sits on the former site of the Foxhead Inn, one of the first luxury hotels to be built in Niagara Falls, later lost to a dramatic fire on New Year's Eve in 1932 .

> **Head southeast on Clifton Hill, left onto the Niagara Parkway, then left onto Heath Lane. The Floral Clock is on the left.**

THE FLORAL CLOCK

14004 Niagara Parkway, Niagara Falls
Phone: 905-357-2411
Online: www.niagaraparks.com

A popular spot for horticulturists and gardeners, this huge, working clock is covered entirely in flowers. The plants are maintained by the Niagara Parks staff, while the clock mechanics are looked after by Ontario Hydro (Hydro-Electric Power Commission). With up to 16,000 plants used to create the design, the clock design is re-worked and replanted twice a year.

Insider's Tip: Free of charge to visit, the Floral Clock dates back to 1950 and when the door to the tower is open, visitors can see its inner mechanics.

> **Turn left on the Parkway; head towards Niagara-on-the-Lake.**

THE NIAGARA PARKWAY

Make your way from the Falls into picturesque Niagara-on-the-Lake by driving this scenic, winding road that traces the Niagara River. The 55 kilometre (34 mile) route offers breathtaking views, and is lined with fruit stands, B&Bs and wineries. Alongside the Parkway you'll find a dedicated recreational trail for pedestrians and cyclists, and with bike rentals easily available in town, it's a great opportunity to get in a little exercise.

> **Brock's Monument is just off the Parkway.**

BROCK'S MONUMENT

14184 Queenston Street, Queenston
Phone: 905-262-4759
Online: www.niagarapark.com

While meandering your way down the Parkway, stop at Brock's Monument, a site built to honour Major General Issac Brock, Commander-in-Chief of British troops during the War of 1812. Brock was mortally wounded during an American invasion, but the battle ended in victory for the British, cementing Brock's heroism in Canadian history. A 235-step spiral staircase in the massive monument leads visitors to a small indoor platform underneath Brock's statue. Porthole windows provide views of the surrounding Niagara region and Lake Ontario.

Insider's Tip: Only open from May until September; the tour is self-guided.

> **Head west onto Niagara Parkway; continue onto Queen's Parade. Fort**

George is on your right.

FORT GEORGE 👀

51 Queen's Parade, Niagara-on-the-Lake
Phone: 905-468-6614
Online: www.pc.gc.ca

A military post that defended Upper Canada against American invasions during the War of 1812, this historic sight invites visitors to step back in time. Guests can watch musket practice, or sample 19th Century cuisine cooked over an open fire. Tours include stops at the powder magazine, the only original structure and the oldest military building in history, plus the refurbished Officers' Quarters and Guard House among others.

Insider's Tip: Considered one of the most haunted sites in Canada, Candlelight ghost tours of Fort George are offered in the spring and summer with special Halloween ghost tours at the end of October.

> **Turn right onto Queen's Parade; continue into town. Nina's is on your right.**

NINA GELATERIA & PASTRY SHOP 🍴

37 Queen Street, Niagara-on-the-Lake
Phone: 289-868-8852
Online: www.ninagelateria.com

Recharge with an espresso and homemade pastry at Nina's, a great little café on the main strip of NOTL that makes everything in-house and without any artificial ingredients. Recently, the shop added sweet and savoury crepes to the menu which are reportedly moving like ... well, hot crepes. Take a bag of sweet treats over to a picnic table at nearby Simcoe Park (named in honour of John Graves Simcoe, the first Lieutenant Governor of Upper Canada).

Insider's Tip: Whenever we're in town, we stock up on the homemade macarons..

NIAGARA-ON-THE-LAKE 👀 🛒

Stroll along Queen Street. Take in the sights and sounds of picturesque Niagara-on-the-Lake, considered the prettiest town in Canada. Gorgeous architecture, serene parks set against the Lake, elegant restaurants and the famous Shaw Festival all make up this charming place, once a British military base for Empire loyalists fleeing the US during the American Revolution.

TREADWELL FARM-TO-TABLE CUISINE 🍴

114 Queen Street, Niagara-on-the-Lake
Phone: 905-934-9797
Online: www.treadwellcuisine.com

Stop for dinner at Treadwell's, one of our favourite restaurants in Niagara. We always make a point of stopping here for at least one meal when we're in the area, and we have never, ever been disappointed. Located in the heart of Niagara-on-the-Lake, tucked a little back from the street, this quaint bistro owned by father-son team Stephen and James Treadwell is always buzzing with both locals and tourists in the know. Featuring carefully prepared, but unpretentious, farm-to-table cuisine and an eclectic, Niagara-focused (what did you expect?) wine list with unexpected and hard-to-find bottles, the service is friendly, thoughtful and polished. A must visit.

Insider's Tip: The restaurant regularly hosts intimate winemaker dinners. Check out the website for upcoming events during your visit.

GHOST WALK TOURS 🔭

126 Queen Street, Niagara-on-the-Lake
Phone: 855-844-6787
Online: www.ghostwalks.com

Niagara-on-the-Lake is said to be Canada's most haunted town, with many of the historic buildings still housing a spirit or two. Even supernatural skeptics can enjoy an after-dark stroll if for nothing more than taking in the fascinating history of NOTL and the legends that come with it.

Insider's Tip: Tours run nightly during peak season, but slow down to weekends only on the off-season.

> *Head east on Queen Street (toward the clock tower). Turn right onto King*

Street, then right onto John Street West. Pillar and Post is on your right.

PILLAR AND POST INN 🛏

48 John Street West, Niagara-on-the-Lake
Phone: 905-468-2123
Online: www.vintage-hotels.com

If you're hankering for a little more supernatural phenomenon — or just like the idea of stepping back in time — turn in at the Pillar and Post Inn, where as some locals suggest, inexplicable occurrences sometimes happen (included in the book, *Ghosts of Niagara-on-the-Lake*). Originally a cannery built in the 1800s, the stately, yet welcoming hotel features 122 rooms decorated in modern country chic, complete with exposed beams and bricks.

Insider's Tip: Have some fun. Play a game of stare-eyes with the portrait of Lt.-Col. John Butler hanging in the lounge.

Notes

Entry Point:

TORONTO

SCENIC & HISTORIC

WEEKEND TOUR

Friday

> *From downtown Toronto the drive will take about 90 minutes to 2 hours without traffic. Take the Gardiner Expressway west for about 5 kilometres (3 miles), continuing as it turns into the QEW west. After about 50 km (31 miles), keep left at the fork to stay on the QEW towards Niagara. Continue another 50 km to Exit 38B Glendale Avenue North towards Niagara on the Lake. Turn left onto York Road, right onto Airport Road, then right onto Niagara Stone Road, continuing onto Mississauga Street. Turn right onto Queen Street, then left onto Gate Street. Follow Gate Street to Front Street,*

OBAN INN

160 Front Street, Niagara-on-the-Lake
Phone: 866-359-6226
Online: www.oban.com

This boutique inn recently fell under the purview of new GM Ian Schulman, who has worked wonders turning this gorgeous spot into a destination getaway of catered hospitality. Modern, inviting rooms, an award-winning and serene spa, and excellent dining room with friendly staff and a creative kitchen all make for a stay worthy of romantic sojourns and all-girls weekends. Chef Jason Dobbie offers a locally-focused, seasonally-inspired menu, and dining room manager Perry Johnson, who balances making guests feel like old friends without being too familiar, has assembled a treasure trove of local wines.

Insider's Tip: Take advantage of Oban's excellently priced packages which vary throughout the year, and usually include spa treatments, dinner and a wine tour.

> *Only a leisurely 10 minute walk, stroll along Queen Street to the theatre.*

SHAW FESTIVAL

10 Queen's Parade
Phone: 800-511-7429
Online: www.shawfest.com

Take in a show at the Shaw Festival, the second largest repertory theatre company in North America. Inspired by the works of George Bernard Shaw, the Shaw Festival was founded in the 1960s and has grown to include plays by Shaw's contemporaries as well. Running from April through October each year, the Shaw Festival takes up four theatres in Niagara on the Lake, the largest being the Festival Theatre on Queen's Parade at the end of the main strip .

Saturday

SONO'S CAFÉ

1494 Niagara Stone Road, Niagara-on-the-Lake
Phone: 905-468-0045
Online: N/A

A greasy spoondesigned to look like a 1950s diner, this unassuming joint located across from a car dealership is the real deal, serving up delicious breakfast sandwiches for just a couple of bucks. Drive-thru is available, and prompt service keeps the line moving.

> *Turn left onto Mississauga Street, doubling back to town. Zoom is on your left.*

ZOOM BIKE RENTALS

431 Mississauga Road, Niagara-on-the-Lake
Phone: 905-468-2366
Online: www.zoomleisure.com

Explore Niagara's scenic landscape by bike. Zoom rents bikes by the full or half day, and also offers one-way trips if you're too tired to cycle back again. There's tons to see and do on two wheels (grab a map when you pick up your bike); our favourite ride is on the trail that runs alongside the Parkway.

> *(by bike) Turn left on Mississauga Street. Turn right onto William Street, left onto Gate Street, then right onto Prideaux Street. Veer slightly right onto the Niagara Parkway Recreational Trail. Fort George is on your left.*

FORT GEORGE 🔭

51 Queen's Parade, Niagara-on-the-Lake
Phone: 905-468-6614
Online: www.pc.gc.ca

Only a short ride from Zoom, Fort George is a military post that defended Upper Canada against American invasions during the War of 1812. This historic sight invites visitors to step back in time. You can watch musket practice, or sample 19th Century cuisine cooked over an open fire. Tours include stops at the powder magazine, the only original structure and the oldest military building in history, plus the refurbished Officers' Quarters and Guard House among others.

Insider's Tip: Considered one of the most haunted sites in Canada, candle-light ghost tours of Fort George are offered in the spring and summer with special Halloween ghost tours at the end of October.

> *(by bike) Head north on the Niagara Parkway Recreational Trail; turn left onto Queenston Street. The Laura Secord home is on your right.*

LAURA SECORD HOMESTEAD 🔭

29 Queenston Street, Queenston
Phone: 905-262-4851
Online: www.niagaraparks.com

Another historically significant figure to emerge from the War of 1812, Laura Secord risked her life by walking 32 kilometres (20 miles) on her own, despite the fact that at the time women traveling unaccompanied could easily be arrested or even shot. The journey took 18 hours through rough terrain and wilderness, but she managed to get word to soldiers who planned an ambush of their own. The home where she lived (and began her extraordinary journey) has been preserved and restored, with tours led by costumed guides.

Insider's Tip: Canadians a bit fuzzy on history are more familiar with the chocolate and ice cream products named in the war-time heroine's hon-our. The treats are available at the Secord home.

> *(by bike) Turn right on Queenston Street. Turn left onto the Niagara Parkway, right onto York Road, then right onto Four Mile Creek Road. Ravine is on your left.*

RAVINE VINEYARDS

1366 York Road, Niagara-on-the-Lake
Phone: 905-262-8463
Online: www.ravinevineyard.com

Having worked up an appetite, stop at Ravine for a wine tasting and superb lunch. Known for producing top-notch, Burgundy-style Chardonnay and Bordeaux-style reds, Ravine is an organic winery that sits on 34 bucolic acres in the Niagara sub-appellation of St. David's Bench, formed when glaciers carved out the Niagara Escarpment. The Lowrey family has grown grapes here for 5 generations, dating back to the 1800s, and that pioneering, farm spirit carries over to the charmingly rustic restaurant which bakes its own bread, grows its own vegetables and raises its own pigs. Just this year, the enterprising family started making dry ciders from locally grown apples and teamed up with a nearby cannery to jar and can their own sauces and produce, so you can purchase components of the dish you enjoyed in the restaurant to take home.

Insider's Tip: Ravine's tasting room, the Woodruff House, was built in 1802 by a settler named William Woodruff, but destroyed during the War of 1812 when the American army burned the entire village in 1814. Woodruff rebuilt it in 1815 and his family lived there into the early 1900s. Blair and Norma Jane (Lowrey) Harber have received an award from Heritage Niagara for their restoration of the historic building.

> (by bike) Turn left onto Four Mile Creek Road. Turn right onto Niagara Stone Road, right onto William Street, then left onto Gate Street. Oban is on your left.

OSPA AT OBAN INN

160 Front Street, Niagara-on-the-Lake
Phone: 866-359-6226
Online: www.oban.com

Head back to the Inn for some well-deserved rest and relaxation at the renowned OSpa. A pool, steam room, plus a wide range of elite services offer the perfect way to recharge after a busy day of touring. (Ask the staff to arrange bike pick-up).

Insider's Tip: Take advantage of Oban's excellently-priced spa packages which vary throughout the year; check the website for details.

NIAGARA-ON-THE-LAKE

Take a stroll around pretty Niagara-on-the-Lake. Gorgeous architecture, serene parks set against the lake, and the many shops along Queen Street all make up this little town, which was once a British military base for Empire loyalists fleeing the US during the American Revolution. Be sure to check out Oliv Tasting Room which features premium olive oils and vinegars. Wine Country Vintners, owned by Andrew Peller, has a wine tasting bar for a quick and convenient sampling of Niagara wines.

> *Turn left on Gate St., turn right onto Prideaux St., turn right onto Wellington St., turn left onto Queen's Parade, turn right onto John St. Two Sisters is on your left.*

KITCHEN 76 AT TWO SISTERS VINEYARDS

240 John Street East, Niagara-on-the-Lake
Phone: 905-468-0592
Online: www.twosistersvineyards.com

Step out for dinner at one of Niagara's newest and most inviting winery restaurants. Pulling up to this impressive estate, you'd think it's been here forever — the country stead of some ancient Ontario nobility — however, this striking winery, and its excellent restaurant, only opened in 2013. Owned by the Marotta family and operated by the two sisters, Angela and Melissa, the only thing stuffy about this place are the huge red chairs set just inside the entrance of the grand hallway. The restaurant is all about family: a welcoming harvest table that stretches down the room can sit either one, large group or plenty of little groups to dine family style, but there are also tables for two or four or six that line up along the windows offering magnificent views of the 76 acres of vineyard (and the namesake of Kitchen 76). The open-concept kitchen makes handcrafted Italian dishes that blend comfort with luxury, including house-made pastas and pizzas, along with seafood and meats.

Insider's Tip: Diners can enjoy the convenience of wine shopping from the restaurant; accommodating servers will package selected wines and deliver them to your table, and have it added to the dinner bill.

> *Turn left on John Street East. Turn right onto East and West Line, left onto Niagara Stone Road, then right onto Niagara Regional Road 81. Turn*

left onto Welland Canals Parkway, right onto Glendale Avenue, then right onto Merritt Street. Stone Mill Inn is on your left.

STONE MILL INN

271 Merritt Street, St. Catharines
Phone: 905-680-6455
Online: www.stonemillinn.ca

Built in 1860 as a cotton mill and converted to the hotel about 10 years ago, this luxury inn has 35 uniquely decorated rooms, all of which feature stone walls and architectural details of the original building. The hotel also has an onsite spa and hair salon to offer visitors a little pampering.

Insider's Tip: The Inn is in the middle of a busy area of St. Catharines, but is conveniently close to the highway and wineries.

Sunday

> *Turn right on Merritt Street, then right onto Glendale Avenue. Turn left on Pelham Road, make a sharp right on Louth Street, then turn right onto St. Paul Street W. Bleu Turtle is on your right.*

BLEU TURTLE BREAKFAST BISTRO

215 St. Paul Street West, St. Catharines
Phone: 905-688-0330
Online: www.bleuturtle.com

Locals rave about this uber popular breakfast/brunch spot we hadn't heard about until scouting for this book. Once the word got out, people *insisted* we include this as a must-visit for a superior, elegantly-casual breakfast. Nearly everything is prepared fresh, from daily baked bread to house-made mayonnaise and spreads, even ice creams.

Insider's Tip: Sunday morning is very busy, so call ahead.

> **Head southwest. Turn left onto St. Paul Street, then left onto Ninth Street.**

Rockway is on your right.

ROCKWAY VINEYARDS 🍷

3290 Ninth Street, St. Catharines
Phone: 877-762-5929
Online: www.rockway.net

Start the day with a round of golf. 9 holes or a full 18, Rockway offers a beautiful course in the middle of wine country, perfect both for beginners and those wearing green jackets. Rockway is also a winery producing a roster of award-winning, reds, whites and Icewines.

Insider's Tip: History buffs and wine lovers would be interested in checking out Rockway's wine museum, which contains artifacts and historical pieces dating back through centuries of winemaking.

> *Turn left on Ninth Street. Turn right onto King Street, left onto Ontario Street, then right onto Church Street. Turn left onto Wellington Street. Wellington Court is on your left.*

WELLINGTON COURT 🍴

11 Wellington Street, St. Catharines
Phone: 905-682-5518
Online: www.wellington-court.com

After a morning on the links, refuel at an iconic wine country restaurant.. This welcoming, casual-fine dining restaurant in downtown St. Catharines is just minutes from neighboring vineyards, and its wine list and regionally-inspired menu highlight that proximity. The restaurant started as a café in the 1980s by Chef Erik Peacock's mother, and he took over the kitchen in the early 90s.

Insider's Tip: Wellington Court also runs Henry of Pelham's seasonal winery restaurant, The Coach House (open May through October).

> *Turn left on Wellington Street, right onto Lake Street, then left onto Welland Avenue, taking the ramp to the ON406 N. Take the QEW toward Toronto, exit 55 to Jordan Road. Turn left on N. Service Road, then left on Jordan Road. Upper Canada Cheese Company is on your left.*

UPPER CANADA CHEESE COMPANY 🛒

4159 Jordan Road, Lincoln
Phone: 905-562-9730
Online: www.uppercanadacheese.com

Surrounded by countryside and vineyards, Upper Canada uses the milk of Guernsey cows exclusively to produce its line of artisan cheeses. Capitalizing on local terroir, the herd is milked daily year 'round, with subtle changes in textures and flavours reflecting the cows' seasonal diet. Cheeses are crafted in a production area in the back and sold in the shop out front.

Insider's Tip: Don't miss the Comfort Cream, a cheese similar in style to Camembert, and utterly delicious.

JORDAN VILLAGE 👬

Wander through the charming and quaint Jordan Village in the heart of the Bench wine country, home to Inn on the Twenty, Cave Spring Estates and a handful of unique boutiques, art shops and restaurants, as well as the Jordan Historical Museum, showcasing the 17th century United Empire Loyalist and Pennsylvania German Mennonite roots of the area.

> Turn right onto Nineteenth Street, veer to the right onto Glen Road, then turn right onto Sixth Avenue. Ball's Falls is on your right.

VINELAND ESTATES WINERY 🍷

3620 Moyer Road, Vineland
Phone: 888-846-3526
Online: www.vineland.com

Plan a leisurely dinner at Vineland Estates on your last stop of the day. From your perch in the award-winning restaurant (voted one of the Top 100 in Canada), watch the sun set over the rolling vineyards with the backdrop of Lake Ontario. Scenes like this are why Vineland has been voted one of the most beautiful wineries in North America. Dating back to the 1800s when it was a Mennonite farm, the original structures still stand. The restaurant is located in the original farmhouse and the stunning boutique and tasting room are housed in the barn, supported with massive wood beams, fully restored in 1999. Known for producing zesty, vibrant Rieslings, enjoy a glass on the restaurant's patio while taking in the sweeping views of rolling vineyards overlooking Lake Ontario.

Insider's Tip: The winery is said to be haunted with the spirit of the farming family's Grandma. We've taken tours there where guests have had odd things happen; ask about these strange occurrences when you visit.

> Turn right on Moyer Road. Turn left onto Victoria Avenue, right onto King Street, then left onto Nineteenth Street. Inn on the Twenty is on your left.

INN ON THE TWENTY

3845 Main Street, Jordan
Phone: 800-701-8074
Online: www.innonthetwenty.com

Inn on the Twenty is a charming, 24-suite boutique hotel in the heart of Jordan Village. A tasteful mix of antique and contemporary decor fill the serene, well-serviced Inn. An adjoining spa makes this an ideal spot for romantic getaways; indeed, there's a good chance you may see a bride or two roaming the hallways. Free wi-fi, parking, and dog friendly suites are available.

Insider's Tip: Traveling with a larger group? Check out the Wine Maker's Cottage or Vintage House.

Notes

Notes

Entry Point:

BUFFALO

SCENIC & HISTORIC

DAY TRIP

> *Once over the Peace Bridge, it should take about 10 minutes to get to Old Fort Erie. Head west on the QEW for about 1 kilometres (1/2 mile), taking a slight right onto Regional Road 124/Central Ave ramp. Turn right onto Central Avenue, turn right onto Lakeshore Road.*

OLD FORT ERIE BATTLEGROUND

350 Lakeshore Road, Fort Erie
Phone: 877-642-7275
Online: www.niagaraparks.com

This is the scene of Canada's bloodiest battleground, where more than 3,000 soldiers were killed and wounded during the War of 1812. Today, history buffs and reenactors flock to the grounds to relive the monumental battles that took place here and shaped Canada's future. Ghost tours are also offered, where visitors can pick a side — American or British — and experience the sights and sounds of the fort under siege.

Insider's Tip: In 1987 an archaeological dig uncovered the remains of 28 American soldiers.

> *Take the QEW towards Toronto, exiting at Sodom Road. Turn right onto Sodom Road, right onto Main Street, then left onto Cummington Square West. Turn right onto Macklem Street which turns into Niagara Parkway. Turn left onto Fraser Hill. Table Rock is on your right.*

NIAGARA FALLS/TABLE ROCK CENTRE

6650 Niagara Parkway
Phone: 877-642-7275
Online: www.niagaraparks.com

After your journey back in time, stop to take in one of the great wonders of the world. From Table Rock Centre you can view the Falls (for free) and stroll along the pathway to get the best vantage points. Table Rock Centre also features a restaurant, food court, washrooms, and shopping.

Insider's Tip: Table Rock is home to Journey Behind the Falls and Niagara's Fury.

> *Turn left onto Niagara Parkway. Turn left onto Clifton Hill.*

CLIFTON HILL

Online: www.clifton.com

A major tourist destination, this strip has all the fun houses, haunted houses, wax museums and novelty museums you could possibly stuff onto one, flashing, neon-lit street. A ferris wheel, glow-in-the-dark bowling, glow-in-the-dark golf, fudge factories, and family restaurants all make up the enticing energy of Clifton Hill.

Insider's Tip: Go online to get passes to attractions which are often featured at a discount.

> **Head southeast on Clifton Hill. Turn left onto Falls Avenue; continue onto Niagara Veterans Memorial Highway. Merge left onto the QEW, exit at Glendale Avenue toward Niagara-on-the-Lake. Turn left onto Glendale Avenue, then right onto Taylor Road. The mall is on your left..**

OUTLET COLLECTION AT NIAGARA

300 Taylor Road, Niagara-on-the-Lake
Phone: 905-687-6777
Online: www.outletcollectionniagara.com

This massive, covered outdoor shopping centre gathers more than 100 brand name stores, a food court and event area which will host local farmers markets. Family and dog friendly, the mall offers complimentary bottle warming, diaper kits and strollers, and while dogs are welcome, whether they are allowed into individual stores is up to each manager.

Insider's Tip: If you lock your keys in the car or need to boost a dead battery, the mall offers complimentary car assistance.

> **Turn left on Taylor Road, following the bend as it turns into Niagara Stone Road. The Garrison House is on your left.**

THE GARRISON HOUSE

111C, Unit 2 Garrison Village Drive, Niagara-on-the-Lake
Phone: 905-468-4000
Online: www.thegarrisonhouse.ca
Directly across the street from Jackson-Triggs winery, the Garrison

Houseis a casual gastro-pub, known for burgers made with locally-sourced beef. The wine list is heavy on Niagara, of course, with a small selection of international offerings.

Insider's Tip: No reservations here. First come, first served.

> **> Turn left on Niagara Stone Road. Turn right onto Mary Street, left onto King Street, then right onto Picton Street. Prince of Wales is on your right.**

PRINCE OF WALES HOTEL 🛏

6 Picton Street, Niagara-on-the-Lake
Phone: 888-669-5566
Online: www.vintage-hotels.com

Save room for dessert and tea at the historic Prince of Wales in the heart of Niagara-on-the-Lake. A landmark hotel that takes up nearly a block on the main strip of Niagara-on-the-Lake, the 150-year-old Victorian structure underwent a full restoration in 1998, returning to its original charm. High Tea is held in the Drawing Room, overlooking the main street, perfect for civilized people-watching.

Insider's Tip: The name honors England's Prince Edward, son of King George V and Queen Mary, who visited in 1901 (Edward became King Edward VIII in 1936).

> **> Turn right on Picton Street which turns into Queen's Parade and the Niagara Parkway. Turn right onto Queenston Street.**

BROCK'S MONUMENT 🔭

14184 Queenston Street, Queenston
Phone: 905-262-4759
Online: www.niagarapark.com

Brock's Monument is a 56-metre column atop Queenston Heights, built to honour Major General Issac Brock, Commander-in-Chief of British troops during the War of 1812. Brock was mortally wounded during an American invasion, but the battle ended in victory for the British, cementing Brock's heroism in Canadian history. A 235-step spiral staircase in the massive monument leads visitors to a small indoor platform underneath Brock's statue. Porthole windows provide views of the surrounding Niagara region and Lake Ontario.

Insider's Tip: Only open from May until September; the tour is self-guided.

> **Turn right onto Niagara Parkway. At the roundabout get onto Portage Road. Turn left onto Stanley Avenue, left onto Ferry Street, then right onto Fallsview Boulevard. Fallsview Casino is on your left.**

FALLSVIEW CASINO 🛒

6380 Fallsview Boulevard, Niagara Falls
Phone: 888-352-5788
Online: www.fallsviewcasinoresort.com

If you're itching to roll the dice, Fallsview is the place to be. Canada's largest gaming facility, Fallsview also regularly features live shows with big-name comedians and musicians. And if you win big, the glass-ceiling galleria features tons of shopping.

Insider's Tip: Security seems to be on top of underage users as we get asked for identification on the regular (or maybe that's just because we look like teenagers).

> **Turn right on Fallsview Boulevard. Turn right onto Murray Street, then left onto Niagara Parkway. Turn left onto Clifton Hill, then right onto Falls Avenue. Windows by Jaime Kennedy is on your left.**

WINDOWS BY JAMIE KENNEDY 🍴

Sheraton on the Falls, 5875 Falls Avenue, Niagara Falls
Phone: 866-374-4408
Online: www.windowsbyjamiekennedy.com

Located 13 stories up, the windowed restaurant takes advantage of breathtaking views of the American and Canadian Falls — although, as you can imagine, window seats are at a premium. Jamie Kennedy is a stalwart of Canadian cuisine and one of the pioneers of farm-to-table dining, gaining celebrity status in Toronto before opening this hotel restaurant in the heart of Niagara Falls. True to his food philosophy, the menu changes to reflect the seasons.

Insider's Tip: The regional wine list has been compiled by Tony Aspler, wine critic and Order of Canada recipient.

> **Turn right on Falls Avenue, then right onto Clifton Hill. Turn left onto Oneida Lane, right onto Murray Street, then left onto Fallsview Boulevard. The Hilton is on your right.**

HILTON NIAGARA FALLS/FALLSVIEW

6361 Fallsview Boulevard, Niagara Falls
Phone: 888-370-0325
Online: www.niagarafallshilton.com

Of all the big hotels in Niagara Falls, we like this one the best. Attached by a covered bridge to the casino, this massive hotel offers clean, modern and spacious two-bedroom suites with views of the majestic Falls. Nothing quite like waking up in the morning to a view of one of the natural wonders of the world.

Insider's Tip: With two towers reaching nearly 33 stories, this hotel can accommodate a lot of visitors. However that can mean long waits for elevators and valet during check out, so plan ahead.

Notes

Notes

Entry Point:

BUFFALO

SCENIC & HISTORIC

WEEKEND TOUR

Friday

> *Once over the Peace Bridge, it should take about 10 minutes to get to Old Fort Erie. Head west on the QEW for about 1 kilometres (1/2 mile), taking Exit 21 for Regional Rd 47 East/Lyon's Creek Road East. Turn left onto Stanely Ave.nue, then right onto Marineland Parkway. Turn left onto Portage Road, then right onto Fallsview Boulevard. The Hilton is on your left.*

HILTON NIAGARA FALLS/FALLSVIEW

6361 Fallsview Boulevard, Niagara Falls
Phone: 888-370-0325
Online: www.niagarafallshilton.com

Of all the big hotels in Niagara Falls, we like this one the best. Attached by a covered bridge to the casino, this massive hotel offers clean, modern and spacious two-bedroom suites with views of the majestic Falls. Nothing quite like waking up in the morning to a view of one of the natural wonders of the world.

Insider's Tip: With two towers reaching nearly 33 stories, this hotel can accommodate a lot of visitors. However that can mean long waits for elevators and valet during check out, so plan ahead.

> *Turn left on Fallsview Boulevard, left at Robinson Street, then right onto Stanley Avenue, continuing onto Thorold Stone Road. Turn right onto Portage Road. Tide and Vine is on your left.*

TIDE AND VINE OYSTER HOUSE

3491 Portage Road, Niagara Falls
Phone: 905-356-5782
Online: www.tideandvine.com

Take a short 10 minute drive from the hotel for dinner. Originally one of the most popular food trucks in the Niagara region, catering to a number of wineries, farmers markets and festivals, Mike Langley (renowned Oyster Shucker) and partner Kat Steeves established this brick-and-mortar, rustic-modern oyster bar in a Niagara Falls strip mall about a year ago. Choose from a seafood-focused menu (don't miss Kat's Clam Chowder) with a pairing from the curated selection of craft brews and local wines.

Insider's Tip: Reserve in advance and ask for a seat at the bar; chat with the friendly staff and watch the pros shuck at inspiring speed.

> **Double back to the hotel. Fallview Casino is across the street from the Hilton.**

FALLSVIEW CASINO

6380 Fallsview Boulevard, Niagara Falls
Phone: 888-352-5788
Online: www.fallsviewcasinoresort.com

If you're itching to roll the dice, Fallsview is the place to be. Canada's largest gaming facility, even if gambling isn't your thing, Fallsview regularly features live shows with big name comedians and musicians. And if you win big, the glass-ceiling galleria features tons of shopping.

Insider's Tip: Security seems to be on top of underage users as we get asked for identification on the regular (or maybe that's just because we look like teenagers).

Saturday

HILTON NIAGARA FALLS/FALLSVIEW

6361 Fallsview Boulevard, Niagara Falls
Phone: 888-370-0325
Online: www.niagarafallshilton.com

Grab a quick buffet breakfast at the hotel, or just a simple coffee and muffin from the onsite Starbucks before heading to the market.

> **Turn left onto Fallsviews Boulevard. Turn left onto Murray Street, then veer right onto Main Street. Turn right onto Peer Street, then left onto Sylvia Place.**

NIAGARA FALLS FARMERS MARKET

5943 Sylvia Place, Niagara Falls
Phone: 905-356-7521
Online: www.niagaragreenbelt.com

Located beside the Niagara Falls Museum, this is the perfect place to pick up picnic provisions — farm-fresh produce or homemade pastries, freshly baked croissants or tempting danish (at the time of this writing, coffee or tea isn't part of the Market, so you may want to bring your own to sip with a locally made treat). Part of the Niagara community for 50 years, market vendors gather every Saturday morning year-round to showcase their local wares.

Insider's Tip: The market also features live music and cooking demonstrations.

> *Turn right onto Ferry Street, left onto Stanley Avenue, then left onto Niagara Veterans Memorial Highway. Merge left onto the QEW, exit at Glendale Avenue toward Niagara-on-the-Lake. Turn left onto Glendale Avenue, then right onto Taylor Road. The mall is on your left.*

OUTLET COLLECTION AT NIAGARA

300 Taylor Road, Niagara-on-the-Lake
Phone: 905-687-6777
Online: www.outletcollectionniagara.com

This massive, covered outdoor shopping centre gathers more than 100 brand name stores, a food court, and event area which hosts local farmers markets. Family and dog friendly, the mall offers complimentary bottle warming, diaper kits and strollers, and while dogs are welcome, whether they are allowed into individual stores is up to each manager.

Insider's Tip: If you lock your keys in the car or need to boost a dead battery, the mall offers complimentary car assistance.

> *Take the QEW towards Toronto. Take exit 55/Jordan Station; turn left onto North Service Road. La Grande Hermine is on your right.*

LA GRANDE HERMINE

North Service Road, Jordan

Driving along the QEW from Niagara towards Toronto, you'll see the slightly spooky sight of a tilting, semi-beached, abandoned, 140-foot ship. Rusted, neglected and decaying, it isn't able to be boarded, but nonetheless attracts thousands of curious gawkers for a closer view, wondering how it got there in the first place. La Grande Hermine (The Big Weasel) is a replica of the largest ship French explorer Jacques Cartier sailed and was built in 1914. Over its lifetime, it was a ferry, a cargo ship, even a restaurant. It was towed to Jordan Harbour in 1997 as the owner was hoping to get the green light to bring it closer to Niagara Falls and turn it into a gambling boat, but he passed away before the licensing went through. It's been sitting and half-floating in the Harbour ever since. In the early 2000s, it was the victim of an arson fire, further adding to the mystique of the "Pirate Ship of Niagara."

> *Head northwest on North Service Road. Turn left onto Victoria Avenue, then right onto King Street. Just Cooking is on your right.*

JUST COOKING

3457 King Street, Vineland
Phone: 905-562-3222
Online: www.justcooking.ca

We first heard about this new restaurant after getting enthusiastic recommendations from several local winemakers. This rustic Italian eatery exceeded our own expectations with a superb menu and wine list, both exceptionally well-priced. The unassuming front makes it easy to miss if you don't keep an eye out. Just west of the Victoria Avenue and King Street intersection, Just Cooking features a nearly all VQA wine list and fresh dishes focused on locally-sourced ingredients.

Insider's Tip: While walk-ins are welcome, we strongly recommend reservations; the restaurant is pretty full most days.

> *Turn right on King Street. Turn left onto Thirty Road, then, right onto Ridge Road East. Turn left onto Mountain Street, then left onto Ridge Road West.*

BALL'S FALLS

3292 Sixth Avenue, Lincoln

Phone: 905-562-5235
Online: www.npca.ca

Ball's Falls is named after the Ball family, United Empire Loyalists who moved to the area in the early 19th century. Part of the land they purchased had two waterfalls — the upper falls and the lower falls — both of which can be viewed from above or below. Nature lovers will also enjoy bird watching and hiking through the conservation area which is now in the care of Niagara Peninsula Conservation Authority.

> *Head southeast on Sixth Avenue. Turn left on Glen Road, veer left on Nineteenth Street. Turn right on St. John's Drive, merge onto King Street. Turn left on Haynes Street, then left on Jordan Road. Take the QEW towards Niagard. Take the Glendale Avenue South exit; turn right onto Taylor Road. White Oaks is on your right.*

WHITE OAKS CONFERENCE RESORT AND SPA

253 Taylor Road, Niagara-on-the-Lake
Phone: 800-263-5766
Online: www.whiteoaksresort.com

Located just off the highway, this centrally located hotel is a great option: clean and spacious with modern rooms, a first class gym, indoor pool and spa. It's also located right across the street from a new Outlet mall for bargain hunters and shopaholics.

Insiders Tip: Professional and accommodating Concierge are happy to arrange a chauffeured wine tour.

> *Turn right on Taylor Road and follow the bend as it turns into Niagara Stone Road. Turn right onto Mary Street. Backhouse is on your right.*

BACKHOUSE

242 Mary Street, Niagara-on-the-Lake
Phone: 289-272-1242
Online: www.backhouse.xyz

Set in the unlikely location of a strip mall is where you'll find Niagara's newest, coolest restaurant. With the look of a modern Scandinavian farmhouse, replete with fur throws, wood piles and animal bone centre pieces, Backhouse is at once sleek and comfy, homey yet industrial. Created by husband-and-wife team Bev Hotchkiss and Chef Ryan Crawford, the inventive menu focuses on "cool climate cuisine," with most components sourced locally and many from the on-staff farmer. Items are so fresh that offerings change daily depending on what's available and in season at the farm.

Insider's Tip: In true Canadiana fashion, guests are served a complimentary roasted marshmallow at the end of the meal, but if you are part of the last seating, guests are invited to the open kitchen to roast their own.

Sunday

WHITE OAKS CONFERENCE RESORT AND SPA 🍴

253 Taylor Road, Niagara-on-the-Lake
Phone: 800-263-5766
Online: www.whiteoaksresort.com

Start your day on a healthy note with a natural fruit smoothie from the juice bar at the Starbucks kiosk, then suit up for a game of tennis or squash at White Oaks' excellent fitness facility. (If sports aren't your thing, you could always opt for a treatment at the hotel's top-notch spa). After working up an appetite, enjoy an indulgent breakfast at Liv, one of the hotel's two restaurants before heading into Niagara-on-the-Lake for the day.

Insider's Tip: Liv serves both healthy and indulgent breakfasts until 11AM. If your game runs a little long, Play Urban cafe starts lunch service at 11, so you won't go hungry.

> *Turn right on Taylor Road and follow the bend as it turns into Niagara Stone Road. Turn right onto East and West Line, then left onto Niagara Parkway; continue onto Queen's Parade. Shaw Festival Theatre is on your left.*

SHAW FESTIVAL THEATRE 🔭

10 Queen's Parade
Phone: 800-511-7429

Online: www.shawfest.com

Take in a matinee at the Shaw Festival, the second largest repertory theatre company in North America. Inspired by the works of George Bernard Shaw, the Shaw Festival was founded in the 1960s and has grown to include plays by Shaw's contemporaries as well. Running from April until October each year, the Shaw Festival now takes up four theatres in Niagara on the Lake, the largest being the Festival Theatre on Queen's Parade at the end of the main strip.

NIAGARA-ON-THE-LAKE

Stretch your legs after sitting for a few hours in the theatre with a stroll around charming Niagara-on-the-Lake. Grab a gelato, fudge or espresso from one of the many shops lining the main street, and be sure to check out Oliv Tasting Room which features premium olive oils and vinegars. Wine Country Vintners, owned by Andrew Peller, has a wine tasting bar for a quick and convenient sampling of Niagara wines. There's lots to see in one of Canada's prettiest and most historic little towns.

PIEZA' PIZZERIA

188 Victoria Street, Niagara-on-the-Lake
Phone: 289-868-9191
Online: www.piezapizzeria.com

The newest restaurant to hang its shingle in the Historic Old Town of NOTL is a welcome addition indeed, featuring Napoli-style pizzas, homemade and wood-fired in a gigantic oven imported from Europe. Bright, laid back, and hopping on most days.

Insider's Tip: House-marinated vegetables on the antipasto plate are a must-try.

> *Turn left on Queen Street. Walk 2 blocks. Prince of Wales is on your right.*

PRINCE OF WALES HOTEL

6 Picton Street, Niagara-on-the-Lake
Phone: 888-669-5566

Online: www.vintage-hotels.com

A landmark hotel that takes up nearly a block on the main strip of Niagara-on-the-Lake, the 150-year-old Victorian structure underwent a full restoration in 1998 to re-create its original charm. Traditional rooms, some of which are pet friendly, will make you feel like you stepped back in time.

Insider's Tip: If you plan to arrive in the afternoon, treat yourself to High Tea in the Drawing Room (reservations required).

Notes

TASTING GLOSSARY

Drinking wine is a true multi-sense experience involving sight, smell and taste.

Sight

The first taste is with the eyes. A careful examination of the colour and density of the wine gives us lots of clues about grape variety, alcohol content and age.

Smell

Then the bouquet which reveals the various components of the wine; firstly the bouquet of the grapes, then the secondly the fermentation process and finally the tertiary aromas resulting from the ageing process.

Taste

Taste is the culmination of the journey. The wine is fully appreciated on the palate, as the full bouquet, body and softness is experienced.

When it comes to the actual words, tasters need to borrow their vocabulary from other areas, including fruits, flowers, spices, nuts, types of wood, or metals. Trying to look for common ground, there are some words expert wine tasters habitually use. We hope the words listed below will help you to write more accurate tasting notes or, at least, to understand better those professional descriptions of wine .

Wine Descriptors

Fruits
apple
apricot
banana
blackberry
bramble berries
cherry
coconut
cola
currant
dates
fig

fruit salad
grapefruit
lemon
lime
muskmelon
nectar
orange
olive
papaya
peach
pear
pineapple

plum
pomegranate
prune
raisin
raspberry
strawberry
watermelon

Nuts
almonds
hazelnut
lichee

pecan
walnut

Flavorings
allspice
anise
basil
beer
black pepper
butterscotch
caramel
caraway
cardamom
chocolate
cinnamon
clove
coriander
curry
dill
garlic
ginger
grenadine
honey
juniper
licorice
marjoram
mint
mustard
nutmeg
oregano
paprika
rye
saffron
sage
sesame
soy
turmeric
vanilla

Misc. Food
beef
bell pepper
bread
broccoli
butter
cabbage
celery
cheddar
coffee
cucumber
dough
fish
ham
honey
kraut
lamb
lettuce
malt
mushrooms
oil
onion
parmesan
parsley
pickles
pimento
pork
rancid
rotten egg
sausage
tea
toast
tomato

Other
alum
ammonia
camphor
cardboard
cedar

damp earth
dead leaves
eucalyptus
glue
grass
hay
leather
matches
metallic
mildew
mold
musk
oak
pertoleum
pine
plastic
redwood
resin
rubber
sandalwood
soap
smoke
sweat
talk
tobacco
wet dog

Flowers
apple blossom
carnation
geranium
jasmine
lilac
rose
violet

Balance
balanced
brittle
clumsy

delicate
fat
flabby
graceful
harmonious
imbalanced
inharmonious
lacy
married
puckery
severe
smooth
supple
taut

Style
aristocratic
arresting
charming
character
classic
compelling
distinguished
dull
fancy
flashy
gulpable
languid
lithe
nervous
peacock's tail
presumptuous
refreshing
savoring
seductive
sensitive
sensuous
sipping
sophisticated
stylish

suave
vivacious
winsome

Evaluative
average
flawless
ordinary
palatable
bad
lackluster
objectionable
poor
appealing
attractive
ethereal
excellent
good
great
lovely
magnificent
mouth or nose
watering
outstanding
pretty
splendid
superior
superlative
tantalizing
triumphant

CALENDAR OF EVENTS

January

Niagara Icewine Festival
Twenty Valley Winter Winefest (Niagara Peninsula)

February

Days of Wine & Chocolate (Niagara Peninsula)

March

Maple in the County (Prince Edward County)

April

Twenty Valley - Get Fresh in the Valley (Niagara Peninsula)

May

Terroir (Prince Edward County)
Terroir Run (Prince Edward County)

June

New Vintage Festival (Niagara Peninsula)
TD Tailgate Party (Niagara Peninsula)
Graze the Bench (Niagara Peninsula)
The Great Canadian Cheese Festival (Prince Edward County)

July

International Cool Climate Chardonnay Celebration (Niagara Peninsula)

September

Niagara Wine Festival (Niagara Peninsula)
Taste Community Grown (Prince Edward County)

November

Twenty Valley - Wrapped Up in the Valley (Niagara Peninsula)
www.20valley.ca/site/wrapped-up

Wassail (Prince Edward County)
www.prince-edward-county.com/wassail

December

Wassail (Prince Edward County)
www.prince-edward-county.com/wassail

ADDITIONAL RESOURCES

Hopefully, you will find this guide fairly comprehensive in our recommended itineraries and places to visit. Should you have any additional questions that can't be addressed by the wineries and their websites, please feel free to visit our website at www.thewinesisters.com or contact us by email at drinkwithus@thewinesisters.com or by tweeting us @TheWineSisters

Additionally, these websites may be helpful for planning your visit:

> winecountryontario.ca
> niagarawinefestival.com
> wineriesofniagaraonthelake.com
> 20valley.ca
> princeedwardcountywine.ca
> vqaontario.ca
> grapegrowersofontario.com

A NOTE FROM THE AUTHORS

Any suggestions, recommendations or new information intended to make this book more complete and user-friendly will be gratefully received and considered for inclusion in the next edition. And, of course, if you find anything in the book you believe to be inaccurate or misleading, we urge you to let us know. Please send messages to:
erin@thewinesisters.com

Notes

Notes

Notes

Notes

Notes

Notes

Notes

Notes

Farm Fresh Books is an independently-owned specialty publisher of cookbooks and travel guides.

Our cookbooks celebrate the food, the people, and the mission of the nation's most enlightened public markets, farmers markets, and farm-to-table restaurants, capturing the grassroots connection to farms and fields and showcasing the bounty and enterprise of community gathering places.

Our travel guides examine what's new, what's enduring, and what's surprising in regional wine country. Thoughtfully-planned, easy-to-follow itineraries inspire and enrich visits to wineries, microbreweries, and along scenic and historic trails — making the most of a one-day jaunt or weekend excursion, including what to sip, where to eat, and where to stay.

Farm Fresh Books
www.farmfreshbooks.com

Made in the USA
Middletown, DE
20 July 2018